Content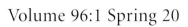

GW00507639

Volume 96:1 Spring 20

Poems

Centrefold

Reviews

Endpapers

POEMS

>   So that
> as they weave, dodge, collide, collapse in breathless
> haystacks – and rise and fall and rise again –
> we're made, if not one, then at least whole.
>   —Alfred Corn

W. S. Merwin
Little Soul

After Hadrian

Little soul little stray
little drifter
now where will you stay
all pale and all alone
after the way
you used to make fun of things

This poem appears in the April issue of *Poetry*.

Les Murray
Recognising The Derision As Fear

Death gets into the suburbs, but sleek
turnover highrise keeps it out of mind

and wilderness, wrapped in its own deaths,
scarcely points us at ours,

but furred rusty machines, and grey
boards unglazed for heritage or holiday –

you can't truck in enough bricks.
Settled country is the land of the dead,

there you are taught love as mourning,
you shop in boarded-up places.

It's great to follow car-dust
out towards the Mistake,

way past a working people's farm,
long widowed, standing in space.

Upright Clear Across

for Kay Alden

It's like when, every year, flooding
in our river would be first to cut
the two-lane Pacific Highway.
We kids would pedal down barefoot

to the long ripple of the causeway
and wade, deep in freezing fawn energy,
ahead of windscreens slashing rain.
We were all innocent authority.

The through traffic was mostly wise
enough not to try our back roads
so we'd draw the North Coast back together,
its trips, its mercy dashes, its loads,

slow-dancing up to our navel
maybe with a whole train of followers.
Each step was a stance, with the force
coming all from one side between shores.

Every landing brought us ten bobs and silver
and a facing lot with a bag on their motor
wanting us to prove again what we
had just proved, that the causeway was there.

We could have, but never did, lose our footing
or tangle in a drowning fence
from which wire might be cut for towing –
and then bridges came, high level,
and ant-logs sailed on beneath affluence.

Allison Funk
Boltonia

It's a fugitive species,
    the botanist explains
as she leads me into a mob of willows,

    giant ragweed and cheatgrass.
Just beyond us, on the great river
    flowing between its levees and dams

a lock lifts a barge with the care
    someone takes to comfort a newborn
and lay him back down to sleep.

    So what if everything's dangerous –
rocks, sandbars, what wakes us –
    aren't those who straitjacket a river

as crazy in their own way
    as a mother who dreams up a pitch-sealed ark
made of rushes to hide her child inside?

    And the son, what becomes of him
after he's grown? Everyone around him
    foreign-sounding, most, he's sure,

plotting his end. Slow of speech anyway,
    fear making him dumb,
he hears the voice of God inside him.

    It's dizzying, this spinning –
mind, a river walled-in,
    stories of bondage and freedom,

even the botanist's vision of seeds
    riding the backs of annual floods
to fill our valley with flowers.

    Every spring now she comes out
to this dry plain to tag the few young plants
    she finds, returning in another season

to look for survivors.
    What they need is that first world
we've lost, she says.

    So late August, how can I hope
to find *Boltonia decurrens*,
    head high with frosty-pink blooms?

Or you, my endangered one
    whom I'm pursuing too
in this bottomland.

Allison Funk was introduced to British readers by John Burnside's essay in *PR* 95:2

Pascale Petit

The Trees Show Their Rings, The Animals Their Veins

after Franz Marc

That clear night, I saw a new kind of painting
on a great black canvas. The moon hung low

as if conducting a colour symphony.

The animals offered their veins as violin strings.
The trees unwound their rings

for dressings to staunch the deepest wounds.

Stars choired over the front line
which flowered with musical notes.

For days afterwards, I carried the constellations
in my head like a fragrant nocturne.

Gerard Smyth
Flood

It must have happened while
my eyes were closed.
The river poured into the town.
The moon turned up the volume of the tides.

Soon sandbags were stacked
like the trench-defences
in *All Quiet On The Western Front*.
Floodwater burst into back alleys

and bits of ground where people
were born, lived, died.
It came through the hall where someone
was singing about *Apple Blossom Time*.

Like the fire in Alexandria,
it surpassed our understanding:
everything destroyed or made
unrecognisable: books and boutique dresses;

the shopkeeper's supply of bread and cheese
and wine, his jars of honey
and the tailor's dummy
like a backstroke swimmer in the Nile.

Ruth Fainlight
Plans

The Aymara people of the High Andes believe that the future is hidden, unknown and mysterious, as impossible to see as the skin in the middle of my back, no matter how I turn and twist. They cannot feel regret or disappointment, because they do not make plans.

But the past is unalterable: a coloured map spread across the floor or a landscape seen from a plane, the chance-discovered photograph of what at first seems just a group of strangers, between the pages of a book, then the thrill to recognise the family face; a phalanx of memories, actions and their consequences, sounds and images manifesting before me, to be contemplated – if I dare to look.

When I stare at the sky on a clear night, I must remember that this radiance has its source sometimes as far away as the edges of the universe – has passed through vastnesses of space and aeons of time (as I have been taught to name such things).

Perhaps no one will be left on earth to see the light the furthest stars now emit. As the past exists in the present, and the future's latent image on the present's silvered surface is only revealed, like film in developer, by being lived, I almost understand (and admire, and wish I could emulate) the Aymaras' lack of surprise when things do not turn out as they expect.

John Kinsella
Forest Encomia Of The South-West

1.
Head State Forester, my grandfather
surveyed jarrah and counted pines
tucked into the hardwood
as soft sell, short shrift,
quick-growing
turnarounds; watched fire
sweep across his fiefdom,
crosscut into ledgers,
health of that jarrah and marri,
blackbutt on the fringe,
named the fastidiousness
of his Scottish wife
Ann Livy Plurabelle,
and made her Irish
where the convolution of sounds
was called "the bush", and dances
at Jarrahdale were as far
away as the hospital.

Kinsella is a road and a forest.
Kinsella is an overlay.
Kinsella is a post-war boom-time
verging on the changing ways.
He died when I was a few years old.
He smoked heavily.
Was tall with a parched face.
My father took me to look at the absent signifier,
the hollow birth-right. The fire-tower,
the ever-ready batteries' cardboard cylinders
still below, the phone smashed by vandals.
Up the fire trail, on the granite summit,

hard-core partying place.
Arsonist incidentals' irony
too good to refuse as the lighter gloats
in high temperature and fuck, man, you've set it off,
can't stamp it out, let's get the fuck out of here.
They don't say a word, ever. But you've
met them in pubs. You've seen the spark
in their eyes, their hatred of forests.

The resinous hardwood I split with an axe
as if under the seared surface
it's seamed;
           from a young age the off-cuts
of his bush upbringing – my father, his father –
where he chopped the finger
off a cousin – a dare on the chopping block –
my father. His father walloped him.

The family from County Wicklow,
foresters there,
foresters here,
a man's man...
and you're Claude's
grandson?
Surprising.

2.
Reportage? When
they came in at Ludlow
they cut the massive open-forest tuarts
and tried farming. That's the 1850s
and there's little talk
of Nyungar people in the forest,
though an artist tells me
there are Kinsellas who are blackfellas,
and I wonder why I've never met them,

heard of them. I want to find them,
for them to find me.

The sand-mining company
has the government in its pocket – this
is a barely renovated cliché –
and in the forest, police,
saying they'd be over the line
along with the dreadlocks and guitars
if the law told them to,
said all you can do
is watch the survey markers.
I ring lawyers. If they go outside
the allotted space... indigenous rights,
rare species, all are collated
in the effort to resist. Failure
allots expediency to the roadside camp
and issues of masculinity: locked on,
boys score points and tally arrests,
the forests goes under, girls
in dungarees call on the moon goddess,
and they move on.

3.
My father, long separated from the forests
of his birth, drives through the wooded country
just for the sake of driving. I like to go up
into the hills, he says. Just to drive.

4.
Surrounded by the paraphernalia of foresting
the cutting and tearing of bark is head over shoulder
in the pit, raining down flaky tears,
an electric rip – of the tongue,
taste not so unlike the taste we have of ourselves,
skin, flesh, chapels in a clearing,

wound sucked dry,
ice-skimmed water baptismally broken,
threads of mist as sunrises and sunsets
suffused are as much as we witness
on open plains, oceans;
never mind the pain
of working bullocks.

5.
Giving the finger to a logging truck
is giving the finger to small-town rage
against heritage imagined as consistency
and moral equilibrium, as connection,
as vacant spaces grind logic into woodchips
and the spout shoots out time sheets.

Giving the finger to a logging truck
is to make the barrelled weight of trunks shift
against the squared U-prongs of praise, offerings-up,
gimleted throats to chain and separate
from the better halves of self; in the blood,
the rush is a drink in a bar that trucks no ferals.

Giving the finger to a logging truck
is a shooting offence, and a get-busted for dope-
carrying offence, and a laying-open of the secret
places retribution comeback getting ahead
making a buck fuck the old-growth lock-up
pent-up release, the swerve of the big wheel

ratio to asphalt and hitch-hiker
stranger danger fallout.

6.
Mettle and impulse are group settlement
nano-probe Borg cube homesteads

rendering karri stands fused with paper
the good word is printed on,
anaphora in keeping accounts.
So lengthy the cordage,
building the State,
O liberty looked out upon
from the tall trees.

7.
Sustainable equals dispossession.
Sustainable equals clear-felling.
Sustainable equals selective picking out of infrastructure.
Sustainable equals dieback.
Sustainable equals balance of payments.
Sustainable equals nice floorboards in parliamentary metonymics.
                              Go where you want with this.
Sustainable equals God at the top of the pyramid, logging
                              companies the next rung down.
Sustainable equals the wood for the trees.
Sustainable equals the log in your eye, the splinter in your sister's.
Sustainable equals ochre rivers and a peeling-back of the layers
        of allegory – extended metaphors all the way to the sea.
Sustainable equals the widened highway and its support services'
                                        flow-on effect.
Sustainable equals the commiserating blocks on the forest's edge
        reaching into the forest bit by bit with the
        environmentally-minded eroding their privilege bit by bit.
Sustainable equals the forest-loving dope-grower who crushes the
        micro with every step, as delicate and caring as they might
        be, introducing weeds as s/he never would with prickly
        pear or rose, the rabbits loving the tender shoots, O
        children of nature.
Sustainable equals dieback trod and trod through by effusing
        bushwalkers infiltrated by bird calls – shocked into
        spirituality by the weather calls of white-tailed black
        cockatoos.

Sustainable equals stars cut out around milling towns, forming the
        southern cross in nation-building recognition of later
        migrant influence.
Sustainable equals forest by any other name.
Sustainable equals election promises come up trumps, couched in
                                                    reassurances.

8.
It's so wet in there: wetter
than anywhere else. A deflected wet
that intensifies, gets under all cover.
In the ice cold you sweat,
and are we under the layers,
the canopy focussing
hard-hitting echoes
on every pore,
clasping undergrowth
too succulent, luring
you in where it's no drier.

9.
Extra-wide gravel roads
deep south so fire won't roll
as smoke so dense
you crawl
slower than through the worst fog
tightened windows preventing
not of the suffocating sting
you associate with those
you love most, love most
in the time left to you,
the pluming crown of flame
as much a vision
as you're going to get.

Carole Satyamurti
If Time Is This Never

this calm continual spill over
the edge of the steep,
river sliding without tremor
without let, over the lip
and down, and more
coming, and more
time for ever

and if there's no firm having
no preserving
from endless drop away
life's blood
all loves, marvels, falling
no holding them
in the cupped heart
no retrieving

then what sense, what ground
is there? All around
the water moves and moves
land liquefies, all forms
mutate – where am I
whose bones even
are made of time
to stand?

Mila Haugová
The Clay Waits Motionless

Memory out of the caves
so near to love...
How mortally not to wound?

What is it to be writing a poem?

To build into oneself
another body?

Woven nest, stone
dwelling, a warm wintering...
A cathedral of a woman from wings' plumage...
A trace in the hair of the Huntress?

Upon my throat
a moist animal touch
(the prey ceases to be
shy), only a hint of blood,
only a tender lasso...

a precisely aimed
shot, always it carries
within itself a part of the one
that did the shooting.

The clay waits motionless for motion

*

from the cradle of stars
into
the syllable of the body
as far as
incommensurability of sharpnesses
above
double-speech double-darkness
between
time present at all velocities
beyond
the discovery of hope
through
the fingers beneath the translucent skin
in
the touch of my touch
alongside
but it's not as simple
into
the mobile boundary

Translated by James Naughton

Moniza Alvi
I Hold My Breath In This Country With Its Sad Past

I hold my breath for fear of saying the wrong thing.

I hold my breath in admiration.

Because everything points to this hinterland –
the generosity of the people
the rawness of the cold
the over-heated rooms
the scooped-out cottage-loaf filled with soup.

And sometimes all talk seems delicately
configured around a silence.

I can't begin to imagine how a whole people
could be so cruelly punished.

Slowly, slowly the present
slips through the hands of the past.

And at the flick of a switch
it is red and not grey that I see
beneath the thin layer of snow.

Up the main street, under the Christmas lights
stalk the wolves, lynxes and brown bears
of the forests, and even they
have thoughts, sorrow and pride.

Mark Weiss
Translated

In exile do you hear
horrible stories from the homeland and
wring your hands? Do you
turn your back and begin to make as they say
a new life?

*

As if body-language had accents,
which it does, the stranger easy to spot
across the field.

But here, watching the Irish barmaid wait for the drink, her arm
folded so that forearm rests against sternum, wrist
curled, her fingers
toying with a necklace.
One would have thought it painful, but the stance
has years of practice behind it,
the line from gesture to dance,
depiction to enunciation.

She spoke the gestures
of her native land.

And that other one did so after three generations.

*

I suddenly find myself imagining
my friends torn, dis-
membered, tortured, nightmares
from the evening news,

and imagine last words,
Carlos taking them down
because I'm beyond writing. "I have always been
a harlequin," I say,
too distracted to find the right phrase.

What kind of legacy would that be,
lucky as I've been,

all the sounds of the world to choose from?

*

Always puzzled by the separation of passion from the everyday.
Impossible to imagine the way instinct could erupt
through such lives, clothing itself
a form of refusal.

*

Even now your lips remember
when they were blossoms.
And I remember when I would say
"Your lips are blossoms."

*

Civilization and its discontents.
It's a matter of degree isn't it.

Complicity's the point isn't it.

*

Two kids on a dark porch
court and smoke and cough
across the street, expecting the night
and its breezes to disperse
whatever evidence.

*

Places named for the words first heard there. So
what I call "pomegranate" you call
"ruddy," or "went," and courtship
becomes the exchange of names.
Smitten, how charming that what you call
"haberdasher" I call
"clout," though we both
swim there. Translating desire,
I reach for "cudgel," that mound
you love me to touch, the left one, and its mate,
"compassion."

*

Every word a sort of conquest.

Douglas Houston
Checked Out

I looked for you round Henleaze, tried the shops,
The ports of call that were your usual stops.
'He is not here,' the cafe lady said,
'I heard he died. They found him in his bed.'

I walked back to the day I saw you last.
I should have know that you were going past
The point of no return, exhausted, racked
With coughing while we talked. I didn't act

To save you, didn't know you'd reached a place
Whence you'd step out of life into deep space.
We shook hands like we always did and I
Drove to my woman's, left you there to die,

With nothing to be glad about, alone,
Unmoved and desolate in the terminal zone.

Yang Lian
The Journey

From Lee Valley Poems

1.
I wake when the wild goose cries   a wild goose crying
thousands of miles away   piercing the darkness
of night's whirlpool

the river turns   a parched man
thinks of a glass's ink-green rim
wingtips sunk in crystal flap coldly   a brittle chill

the hourglass   anchors every house to the street
after rain tyres slash long bandages from the road

I listen to the boats in my body
jostling against each other   the keels fused into one
when the wild goose cries   the city stuck to your eardrum
flies and hangs elsewhere   a geography light as a wreck

2.
                              water has no meaning
the river turns   the wind rasps against dry hulls
rats love climbing the davit struts
the sharp tang of rust   an exquisite fish-bone
moonlight paints a full arc   making-up a corpse's face
quiet as a wooden womb thrown on the bank
a little way from the water's lapping   a little way from the gravel
a little way from the rudder which has escaped all bearings among the stars
the oars drawn in like tired questions
bound in a stranglehold around the axle

water has no meaning
but on the porcelain of the water's surface   the marina's glaze is fire-painted
time brings the theme of memory
what can a boat cradled by air remember
except to hear   the dense embroidery of water
except to be a bell   ringing to delete
to delete the engraved ear   the ceaseless migrations
but earth falters
the criss-crossed light-years around the nest
no longer know   who sails on what river
water   sinters into a crust of shatterproof porcelain
long broken   fissioning one and every night
fissioning history which so loves to compose

water has no meaning   therefore
a terror of raising the periscope
is wakened in the abandoned boat   is wakened and peeps
at the sky where billions of orbits clutch lotuses
all close their coral colours   when they whisper
they are clutched by a grammar which has no past   no nostalgia
the iron organs submit to their internal vacuum
how long can they survive   when fish purposefully seek the poison in oxygen
what more can they possibly find   in front of an unblinking eye
dawn doesn't have to arrive   dawn has already swum elsewhere
an aesthetics cut to the quick   a little way from
desolation

where the wild geese cry is the underwater
co-ordinate   where a corpse can continue the journey that ended last night

3.
the circle's centre   a text secretly watching me
draft another page
the circle   a bed floating in a ghost's script
exposed by water and cancelled by water

did the wild geese really cry   or is the night so deep it's become timeless
the wild geese's arched and chopped necks
the more afraid I am to listen the easier it's summoned

hearing metaphorizes landscape   darkness
metaphorizes matter that confines me
the city's hydromechanics splash out a branch of peach-blossom
the hammering heartbeat   still withholds the horizon

a brain metaphorizes the starry sky   the bed-edge
metaphorizes the boat's side
a scream locked in a raindrop   the pull of dreams
longing for each other over thousands of miles
all in the circle   driven out by what isn't yet written

circle back to here

Translated by Pascale Petit

For Yang Lian's essay on the context of 'The Journey', see page 72.

Paul Batchelor
According to Culpeper

Whose tender demand
        makes the hawthorn bend
                & sunlight concede

a sweet inhaling
        finer than honey,
                a narcotic soft

as babies' breath
                & summary justice
                        according to Culpeper

for headaches, breathlessness,
        sleepless nights & all
                        manner of affections of the heart?

For answer, see contributors' notes.

Paul Muldoon
Two Lyrics: (1) See If I Care

I caught this big ticket item
At the Spotted Pig
She said I don't know you from Adam
I said see if I give a fig
I don't give any credence
To your idea of Eden
So see if I care
See if I care

She said you know there's no tour
Of the bosom of Abraham
I said frankly my dear
I don't give a damn
I still have my Coke and Fanta
Shipped in from Atlanta
So see if I care
See if I care

See if I care if you're that former lover
Who's now a high flyer
In homeland security
See if I care if you've gone undercover
And you're wearing that wire
Because you're checking to see
If I care, baby,
Just checking to see if I care

She said you must be miffed
About crossing the Acheron
I said don't think I'm unmoved
Just that I've moved on
There's a fresh crop of ladies
Over here in Hades
So see if I care
See if I care

(2) Meat And Drink

No more crouching round a campfire
With Sangria and samphire
No no no no no
No more hanging out with mobsters
Over Lambrusco and lobster
Fra Diavolo

When you're all I need, don't you see,
You're meat and drink to me

No more *frites* with fashionistas
No *insalata mistas*
No nights on the tiles
No deep-dishing with designers
Now closing the Munson Diner's
Going out of style

I'm through with jumping in the sake
With Kenzo and Miyake

I'm done with Valpol and polenta
With Oscar de la Renta
Now the joint is pastry-cased
Enough of the *modus vivendi*
Of Ferragamo and Fendi
No mooching through Balducci's
With Pucci and Gucci
Finding nothing to my taste

When you're all I need, don't you see,
You're meat and drink to me

No more takeout with screenwriters
Still pulling their all-nighters
When they're thirty-eight
No more blind dates with day traders

Nut-butting corporate raiders
My appetite to sate
No more schmoozing in-house shysters
Pork-rinds and Jaegermeisters
Now you're on my plate

When you're all I need, don't you see,
You're meat and drink to me

'See if I Care' and 'Meat and Drink' are lyrics for RACKETT who, according to
their website, play "three-car garage rock": www.rackett.org/

Petr Borkovec
Sonograph

for Franz Hammerbacher

A thrush up on the gutter
– still spreading and already drying out –
like a blot of ink in bold. I flexed
a forking wand of walnut, an antler
still hooked onto a ringing head,
and it came springing back at me
as though still on the tree.
I looked for skulls in all the leaves
and bones of stalks. The thrush sang.

Teams combed the alders near the river.
The stains left after branches tilt
in the wind. They fleck and gather
in the dry wind. A golden worm,
it seems, works through the facing shore.
Small bits of driftwood flock and cloud
along in front of a dead carp,
which in its turn, eye clouded over,
snags in the shoulder of the river

where branches burn: they blossom
like in a documentary, the flames
of fire in daylight with no smoke or sound;
ash swarming up; the glow burgeoning.

Odd shells and old ceramics
turn brightly green amidst the mud
that's full of seeds. Streams of magpies
along the silt and swirls and streaks.
A barge pulled up on to the beach
has rusted into silence;
a thresher's belt, carefully caught
among the lower wheels and cracked,
toys with the thought of starting up again.

The thrush sang all the while.
Against the twilight, now up on the gable.
That metamorphosing stain, I thought,
is almost like a bird – it looks like one.
But everything flowed into it.
And the song was still unchanging.
I watched. Called everything the same.

I listened. The thrush sang.
I believed it all. What it seemed. How it looked.

I Pick Up After Bishop

Down at the water's edge, at the place
where they haul up the boats, up the long ramp
descending into the water, thin silver
tree trunks are laid horizontally
across gray stones, down and down
at intervals of four or five feet.

As though it will never move again,
clamped by flowing water, to the left
it stands, branches grown over the watermark,
and bits of board that weeds have caught hold of,
a lumber boat, its coat of yellow
slowly grading into rust.

Above the dusty bow, above the cone
of smooth rocks which supports
a platform on the far end, as though hung in mid-air,
with a conveyor belt, there stands
an articulated jib with half-turned scoop
in which rainwater shines like oil.

A track runs to the sawmill in the field,
straight and roasted hard as bricks,
and there it turns and skirts it
in four rounded angles,
and stretches off across the fields,
beaten, straight and exact.
Up from the river, on the opposite bank,
vertical and smooth as a wall, the rock rises.
Pines sway languidly,
and in between these, through wide breaks,
other pines unfold,
these a little higher, on the grassy top.

Translated by Justin Quinn

The Geoffrey Dearmer Prize:
Andrew Bailey

Ideally I'd like the poem to be a thing that works like a charm, literally, to lead you a little astray, a little further away from me. What first sold me on poetry was the weightless feeling when words pick you up by the way they're arranged – whether that's rhetoric, magic, hypnosis, spin – and that feeling, I suppose, is what I'm trying to recreate. And hide behind.

Super Flat Poem

No background, baby, no backstory,
            nothing to look forward to,
                        I'm only here to smile,
smile at you peaceful
            in a field of flowers, field as in
                        field of colour, and all the flowers smile
in many colours
            behind this smiling me, bunny ears
                        perked up happy. Smile, your smile
is a gift for me as mine for you is,
            and we shall share back and forth
                        the same instance of smile –
we are mirrors with a smile between,
            only here in as much
                        as we are seen. Look into the smile,
see 'into' as the illusion
            of bouncing back. Although darker
                        at one edge you are not round – the smile
does not diminish, so the mirrors
            share a plane, and where planes coincide
                        no light does. And the smile
must have no depth then, must be
            on both our faces, which are one face
pressed flat to nothing, no-one to see it,
            nothing behind pushing all
                        to a wafer of nothing but smile.

Snow

Over the hills comes the song of the clouds singing hope for us:

we will bring snow, bring snow soon, but have all of you hope,
hope just so much harder and it will be all of you, all,

that bring us benevolent, snow in our hearts, and have it fall over you,
fall over hedges and ditches, furrows and roofs, like clouds on the
                                                        ground

for that is what it is, our hearts drawn out and refrosted for you,
for the ground, and all round your snuggling gloves and boots

will be airquilted ice compacting to blankets then softening
to spring, it will do, we promise, and all you need do is hope harder.

What else can bring you the water you want? You need us,
you know this, and still we must tell you and tell you until you believe.

Now cross your mittened fingers, squeeze up tight your booted toes,
and stand scrunched and still, with everything taut with hope, and hope.

ℬ

Peter Sansom
Poem

I'd heard about the man who, drunk, stood up
and said, This is where I get off, then opened
a moving door and jumped. A friend
of a friend pulled the communication cord.
It came to mind and I told the story, and then
this person remembered standing next
to a boy who lowered the window,
and stuck out his head. Decapitated,
was all she said. But I saw a guillotine
and the torso turning back, going on
like they say a chicken does, and this person
stepping aside to let the boy go
wherever it was he last thought he should go.

Conversation:
Arrowing in

Robert Crawford (1)
The Junction

Now I know how as I loped alone in the cold along Brownside Road,
Down and round Stonelaw Road, each road was a coded
Loop or lap in that map of hand-me-down walks
My dad did daily. I know as I dodged where vans shot
Round Wellshot Drive or down Douglas Drive, bowling
Past Cambuslang Bowling Green, I know now
How, as the treads of my brogues trod untarred Myrtle Walk,
Know as I slowly strolled down lanes in the rain, as you
Ran against the wind, against the clock past Rockhampton Avenue down
                                        Westwood Hill,
Windchill at your back – you know now too, as you turned into Burns
                                        Park, know how

As you carried messages from Melbourne to Tasman
To Maxwelltown Avenue – we now know
As we went our own ways, each miles away, our feet
Still growing, still walking, as we ran, as we bathed our feet,
You in East Kilbride, I in Cambuslang, you in the Plaza, I in Nevada,
You in Paris, on Harris, in Chester, in Sheffield, on Sauchiehall Street,
I in Broad Street, near Broadford, on Bar Hill, at Boar's Hill, through
                                        Boarhills,
We were hurrying on
Towards the intersection of Rutherglen Road with the Rue de Rivoli,
The junction of Tillie Street with Zurich's Banhofstrasse, of Newmill
            Gardens, St Andrews, with Laramie's Rogers Canyon Road,
To where the Main Street in Burnside, Glasgow, joins the main street in
                                        Burnside, Fife,
Passing through ourselves, to ourselves, we knew ourselves
Heading towards a husband, a wife.

Wayne Burrows
The Protein Songs

In science, as in the rest of life, the paths are paths only in retrospect...in
the tree of life itself there seems to be play in the system: what look like
swerves and random branches.

> Jonathan Weiner, *Time, Love, Memory* (1999)

(i)
In the word is a beginning,
a fragmented alphabet,
a dish of peas or bottled flies,
a tray of printer's metal type,
a John Bull rubber-stamping kit
with half the letters missing
and no full-stops:

agctcgctga, gacttcctgg...

Now a single silver disc
whirrs, unreels
three billion chemical base pairs,
a scroll of letters, *a-c-t-g*,
expansive as the biosphere,
its flows and anagrams, chants and drones,
unravelling the names of Sumerian gods
in the electronic bowl
of a laptop-drive –

agctcgctga, gacttcctgg...

like an overture.

(ii)
Here are the song-line's component notes,
scrawled in the margins
of a petrie dish
where phage is eaten by viruses,
spores proliferate, fruit-flies swarm,
fungi, mould and nematodes
spread through moisture, cultures,
ascending orders and taxonomies;

> *Eukaryota,*
> > *Metazoa,*
> > > *Chordata...*

links the wave of frogs that surges up
from tidal pools
with the storm of locusts, the shoal of fish,
the handful of wheat-seed
with the nest of ants,
the bramble, dragonfly, onion, owl;
joins beetle to blue whale,
lizard to cormorant and spider's web:
in toads and water
and *Phycomyces* we trace our names.

(iii)
There are songs in the darkness,
voices, harmonies, rounds.
There are moon and stars and candlelight
where women in night-gowns
gathered around an open tent,
find unison as the warm night air
drifts in from the sea
and twelve voices climb an ascending scale:

> *Craniata,*
> > *Vertebrata,*
> > > *Euteleostomi...*

The notes – A, G, C –
rearrange like genes in a chromosome,
change the shape
of the melody with every breath
to a different song,
the breath itself to random words.
The human voice, singing to and of itself
as it evolved itself to do:

> *Mammalia,*
> > *Eutheria,*
> > > *Primate...*

(iv)
But what evolves?
> > The kora player in next-door's yard,
tickling rivers from strings and a hollow gourd,
breaks the heart more easily when the dusk sets in
than the multi-tracked choir inside the CD machine.

(v)
Still, the heart recovers, cell by cell,
and the heat of the sun, now stored in her naked back,
abandons itself to the stasis and pulse
of cicadas, fire-flies and insect-wings
in the air outside. Grapes hang, molecular, on twisted vines.
Each unripe sphere ascends its stalk
on a programmed course:

> *Catarrhini,*
> > *Hominidae,*
> > > *Homo.*

We reach our end in breathing,
in protein songs that spill into flesh,
the miniscule shoals of fish
that run their patterns just below the waves
like code in a laptop, a compound in blood.

(vi)
What we remember, faintly,
in this deep blue hour
far from beginnings – the world's, and ours –
is how to open, turn, recall ourselves
up to our ribs in a crystal sea
where shredded ribbons of seaweed
like audiotape
form vast, dark slicks
and the evidence of three billion years
washes in on the tide.

(vii)
And now the winds return –
the genome's *Torah* is chanted plain
as a choir of scholars in a thousand labs worldwide
programme machinery to extract one word
from all creation,
the lines of a ragged, unsettling song:

agctcgctga, gacttcctgg...

What we have been is now written.
What we become remains blank.

The Protein Songs were commissioned by Retina Dance Company for use in the
performance *Eleven Stories For The Body, Distance To Our Soul.*

Julian Stannard
Rome-Crotone, 2005

I take an uneasy drink at the *Caffé Greco*
then board a train for the South.
The accent's thickening
like the thighs, the children, the dust.
The good world's gone...

I find a place in the dining car:
the pain of Naples drops behind a sunset.
The waiter smiles, handing me
a wine that's spiked in blood.

Woozy now, I haul my cases off at *Poala*
and stand an hour at the bar.
I eat a slice of last year's panettone,
the picture of Padre Pio sets my teeth on edge.

We are continents away from Rome,
those Japanese who stabbed me with their maps.
The train limps, stops, quickens.
Figures are laid out in complicated sleep.

My brother's body's broken off the coast of Thailand,
I'm arrowing in on death.

Michael Schmidt
Notes For The Cactus Poem

The teddy bear cholla and the fat fat

Oh buckthorn, devil, whipple, teddy bear

Oh beavertail, oh pancake, porcupine

Oh plump saguaro with your hairy arms, I love
Each of you with a different nerve of heart.
Especially you, so buxom, pert, your birds
Cupped in your pits and crotches, little friends

Oh areoles and aureoles, the orioles
With yellow caps are havering and hot
Making themselves a breeze with their cut wings

I ask the docent and he indicates

Oh nation, how you might have been, spread from
So sure an order, with such tendering love

Alfred Corn
Fútbol

As if to move a flexible sphere from here
to there with unassisted head and foot
were natural and obvious. As if
a dance could always bow to resolute
constraint and never be danced the same way twice.
As if whistles and cheers, the hullabaloo
of fervent gazers were all the music needed
to keep its players' goals in tune. So that
as they weave, dodge, collide, collapse in breathless
haystacks – and rise and fall and rise again –
we're made, if not one, then at least whole.

John Hartley Williams
Donkey Jacket

Reversed it's a bullfighter's cape.
It's the cloak of Sir Francis Drake,
made to be swung & dragged along the ground
for small feet to crush.

A coat
smelling of tarpaulins,
thrown across trucks
in rain...

Coming towards you, opening...
Outer Melton Fabric 65% wool 35% Viscose
A hand rummaging you...
Quality Nubuck Collar
The deep smell of wet wool...
2 Secure Button-down Front Patch Pockets.

This is the coat of the man
you saw on the down escalator,
his wrist stamped
with a blue number, like a pig.

Reinforced shoulders,
sailor-stitched arms & armhole seams,
a treatise on insurrection
in the pocket...

Breast fabric
soft as the navy.

Amarjit Chandan
Wear Me

Wear me
I want to rub against every part of your body
Make me your necklace
I want to be close to your jugular

Wear me
As the sound wears the word
As the seed wears the skin
As the book wears the touch of hands
As the sea wears the sky
As God wears worlds
Wear me

Translated by the author and John Welch

Matthew Sweeney
No Sugar

Sitting, upright, on the sofa,
sandwiched between a pair of twins,
both blond, both beautiful,
wearing the same red leather
miniskirts, the same faces,
the same green sparkling eyes,
I find myself thinking of melon,
green-fleshed, cool from the fridge,
sliced cross ways in half,
the seeds scooped out, the hole
filled with chilled Sauternes.
A cough emanating from one twin
is echoed by the other. I chuckle,
they chuckle in stereo, and outside
the streetlight comes on, a dog
howls, a car alarm starts to blare,
while in this white-carpeted room
the newly-permed mother arrives
with a silver tray, on which sit
three delicate china cups, each with
its leaf-patterned saucer, a tea pot
escaped from Shanghai, a jug
with a peacock on it and milk
of some kind inside. But no sugar,
not a single solitary grain.

Penelope Shuttle
from Missing You

1
This year no-one will ask how you voted,
or if you know the way to town

No-one will call you as an eye-witness
or teach you how to train a bird of prey

No-one will bring you your New Scientist,
try to sell you double-glazing
or tell you their secrets

People will write to you
but you won't answer their letters

The high sheriff of mistletoe
will never catch your eye again

No-one will peel apples for you,
or love you more than you can bear

No-one will forget you

2
I wept in Tesco,
Sainsburys
and in Boots

where they gave me
medicine for grief

But I wept in Asda,
in Woolworths
and in the library

where they gave me
books on grief

I wept in Clarks
looking in vain for shoes
that would stop me weeping

I wept on the peace march
and all through the war

I wept in Superdrug
where they gave me
a free box of tissues

I wept in the churches,
the empty empty churches,

and in the House of Commons –
they voted me out of office

3
I can't cry anyone's tears except my own,
can't teach anything but my own ignorance

I can only fall from my own mountain,
ledge by ledge

I can't rival the wasp's sting
or sew except with my needle

Like a saltwater wife,
I prise open the oyster of my loss,

hoick out the pearl of your death

4
The rainbow is not enough,
nor the flood

My eye can't see enough,
nor my ear absorb sufficient silence

January is not enough,
nor June

Books are not enough
nor the El Grecos

Christianity is not enough,
nor Judaism

China is not enough,
nor India

Good luck is not enough,
nor absolution from the bad

Jasmine is not enough,
nor the rose

Kingdoms are not enough
nor the oldest city in the world,

without you

10
I make my home in your absence,
take your smallest hope

and make it grow

I wake to the dusk of everywhere
as if assisting at my own birth

or arriving in a country
where all the rivers settle down to be ice

11
World was one word
I could not guess it

World was one gesture
I could not copy it

World was one question
I couldn't answer it

World was one song
How could I sing it?

World was one forest
I couldn't fell it

World was one bridge
How was I to cross it?

13
My tamer of doves,
my alphabet of the moon,
fool of night,
harvest's welcome, the grief
of day, my blind man
and my seer,
dreamer against his will,
my furious saint,
warrior of peace

16
Think of me
as a small backward country
appealing for aid from the far-off first world

Imagine the dirt of my shrines,
the riddle of my dry rivers,
the jinx of my cities

When you hold the full purse of autumn
or celebrate the nativity of a pear,

picture me as the hawk of spring,
a one-pupil school,
the safe-keeper of sunrise

Think of me without you,
stuck here forever between rainless May
and the drought of June

17
Your name didn't change
after your death –
many others also answered to it

After your death
the climate didn't change,
the government stayed calm

Waterfalls
remembered you forever,
remaining loyal,
looking for you everywhere,
storm after storm, teacup after teacup

18
Autumn fans its tail without you
and spring bears its burden alone

Summer, that small supernatural being,
manages without you

and winter closes your many doors

Like an interval between kings,
the year is a confusion of reds and golds,

but in the gulag of August
days are where you left them,

nights,
the same

21
I've lived with your death for a year,
that despot death, that realist,

stunned,
as if I've just given birth to a foal,
or made an enemy of the rain

All at once
you had more important things to do
than to live

Death is the feather in your cap,
the source of your fame,
my darkest lesson

This dropout year closes,
I begin my second year without you,
just me and the paper-thin world

Robert Crawford (2)
Shetland Vows

I swear by the unfallen broch of Mousa,
I swear by fallen Snarravoe on Unst

That it is possible to rise above them
Over the rainbowed green nub of The Knab,

And sense, way out at earth's circumference,
Sceptical London, Laramie, Hong Kong

Who doubt the arctic tern-packed broch of Mousa
Or Snarravoe on Unst are as they are,

But, knowing such disbelief, go on believing
In voes and fluff, in monuments and rain

Below the wing's pale rind, and keep faith both
With the soaked planet's whole revealed horizon

And with home ground, the national smudge of Scotland
That holds my wife, our daughter, and our son.

Ioana Ieronim
Descantece:
Traditional Romanian Charms

He got up in the morning
in the singing of songs
in the break of dawn
in the odour of flowers.
He got up from his golden bed
stepped on the silver threshold.

He met The Women.
They took him in their hands,
high up they lifted him,
to the evil wind threw him,
wounded the heart in him.

*

With garlic I'll season you,
with a comb I'll undo you,
and into the fire
I'll throw you.

With nine knives cutting
with nine towels wiping
with nine brooms sweeping.

With nine shovels with nine spades
nine troughs nine forks
with nine sickles with nine rakes
with nine brooms little brushes.

Where are you going, where are you hurrying,
enchanters, enchantresses
wondering men and wondering women
jealous men and jealous women
dragons, dragonesses
lions and lionesses?

*

Weak hour
white hour
blackened hour
snake hour:

from the threshold you jumped into the house
from the threshold you jumped onto the table
from table to plate
from plate to spoon
from the spoon my boy swallowed you
and he fell ill.

*

River-bed to river-bed,
up nine riverbeds,
nine riverbeds far I pushed you
in the tail of the seas I put you

into the sea I threw you,
there to perish and more than perish
like dew in the sun
like spit on the road.

From dust you came, to dust you return.
There's a ladder of riches,
there are barrels of little coins.
Leave the body of my son.

> *Run run run run*
> *Run hollow sun*
> *Lest I reach you*
> *With hollow straw.*

*

Water, water,
as you wash mud from banks

and rust from stones:

wherever you find evil
draw it out,
wherever you find wounds
wash them, heal them.

Put him together,
put his flesh together
like an egg,
fat, white and complete,
so my boy grows rosy,
fat and fruitful.

*

Let evil leave him
like dew in the sun
and sea foam.
For on the day he was born
he had no needs,
he remained in sleep and in the Lord.
And he remained clean
full of light
like sieved gold
he remained in sleep and in the Lord
he covered his flesh and bones in health
like honey covered in the bee-garden,
and basil in the garden.

> *O Mother of God, Sainted Mary,*
> *let there be healing from the Mother of God*
> *and from this Holy day.*

*

There shall not be left to him
so much as a poppy seed
divided into seventy-seven,
thrown in the sea.

*

Four for me
and four for you.

Shining, clean
like flower dew at day break,
like the tears of the eyes
on Holy Mary's hem,
Holy Mary eternal.
Like his mother when she gave birth to him
when he was born on the earth.

A white bird flew over our boy,
the bad charm broke in four,
not even a dry poppy seed
split in four
thrown into the bottom of the sea,
not even that remains.

> *The charm from me*
> *the healing from God.*

These charms and portions of charms have been collated and translated from several published sources.

Translated by Ioana Ieronim with Clare Durey

Myra Schneider
Naming It

As if they are paper cutouts which a giant hand
has crushed on a whim all the buildings around me
buckle and collapse. When the dust settles

a hard white sun is crawling over
a wasteland of broken stone, a single column
is holding up half a triumphal arch. I peer

into a tower whose darkness is packed
with air that smells of decay, pass pink-
headed ranks leading lesser weeds

over tumbled masonry. Here's a slice
of house with layers which could be bedclothes
or fishing nets dangling from the upper floor.

Skirting a seashell bath mapped with cracks,
I search the ground for evidence. Not a hint
of human remains. The panic is all in the rubble.

I pick my way past a yanked tree,
try not to touch grievous roots
grappling with the air. Then I come upon it:

a pool of taintless blue which is so small
I could hold out my hands and cup it.
It's crucial to capture the exact word for its colour:

not azure, aquamarine, cobalt, sapphire.
Soon I'm uttering wildflowers in a litany:
speedwell, bugloss, vetch, forget-me-not.

I stop at harebell trembling on its wiry thread,
harebell that bends but keeps its head.
Babbling its name, I surface in another reality.

Almàssera Vella

Poetry/Creative Writing Courses 2006 Programme

Mountain view from Almassera 2004 – Sue Whitmore

April 22– 29	Julia Stoneham – 'Writing for Radio'
May 27– June 3	Terry Gifford – 'Mountain Walking and Writing'
June 10 –18	Christopher North – 'The Writers Notebook'
Sept. 9 – 16	Tamar Yoseloff (Poetry School) – 'A Paean to Place' Poetry
Sept. 23 – 30	Matthew Sweeney (Poetry School) – Poetry in a Spanish Fiesta

£435 (for 7 nights) all inclusive (exc. flight and insurance). Inspiring environment. Pool, mountain views, 3000 book library – private rooms. Airport pick-up and return.

To secure a place please forward a £50 deposit (cheques to 'Pemberton North SL) to the address hereunder)

ALSO RETREATS from **£150** per week self-catering with access to library, pool and grounds.

A place designed for writers

Other courses planned: Walking, Cookery, Painting

Christopher and Marisa North
Almàssera Vella
Carrer de la Mare de Deu del Miracle 56
Relleu 03578 - Alicante SPAIN
(0034) 966 856003 oldolivepress@tiscali.es
http://www.oldolivepress.com

CENTREFOLD

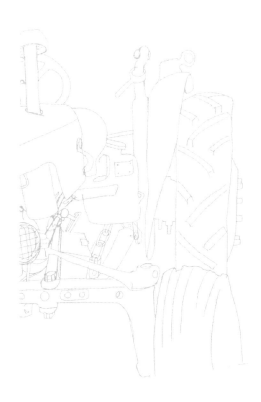

A soul cake, a soul cake, a soul cake.

Dodola and Peperuda:
Balkan Rainmaking Customs

RICHARD BURNS

In a few eastern and south-eastern areas of the Balkans, especially Bulgaria, the rainmaking rite is still practised, even though vestigially. In other parts of the Balkans, the custom has all but died out, although as late as the 1960s it was very much alive in parts of Yugoslavia too, and well-documented by camera-toting ethnologists and travellers in Serbia and Vojvodina:

> The *dodolas* [...] are still very much alive in people's memories [...] whenever there is a drought in summer, the older women wish for the *dodolas* to appear, firmly believing even today in their magical power to make rain. In the village of Brestać in Srem, the last time *dodolas* appeared was in 1988.[1]

During a period of spring or summer drought, it was the custom in many Balkan villages for a group of local girls to undress and then put on various combinations of leaves, sprigs, blossoms, flowers and herbs to perform the rainmaking ceremony. Early reports, made mostly if not entirely by male observers, describe these girls as "naked" under their clothing of greenery: although what precise degree of undress this "nakedness" really constituted is a moot point, since none of the commentators is likely to have witnessed the actual disrobing, let alone the training, preparation or rehearsal of the girls for the ceremony – roles which seem to have been reserved exclusively for mature and sometimes elderly women. At any rate, led by an older girl or young woman who had also been dressed or decorated in this way, the girls then went in procession through their village, and stopped in front of houses to perform dances and sing songs, which included formulaic refrains, all the while calling upon the heavens to send down rain. The housewives poured water over the leader of the troupe, and sometimes the girls themselves sprinkled water over the courtyards, using bundles of sprigs and leaves. They were then rewarded by

1. Bosić, Mila, *Godišnji obicaji Srba u Vojvodini* [*Annual Customs of Serbs in Vojvodina, Novi Sad & Sremska Mitrovica*], 1996, p. 341. See also p. 345: "The *dodolas* more or less entirely disappeared in Vojvodina only after the 1960s, probably as a result of the economic development following the Second World War, including [...] the mechanisation of agricultural work and improvements to fields resulting from the construction of ditches and land-drainage, all of which made crop-production possible on a world-scale. Moreover, the rapid increase of education and culture in the population resulted in the loss of many customs and beliefs in magic, including the *dodolas*." Extracts tr. Vera Radojević & Richard Burns [RB].

the householders with flour or food and sometimes money.

In some areas, especially Dalmatia, Albania and Northern Greece, boys or youths were involved as performers.

The custom – or groups of customs – seems all the more interesting in that, while it flowered predominantly in south-east Europe, typologically comparable elements can also be traced much further north, for example among other Slavs, and possibly among Balts, Teutons and Celts.[2] Moreover, even in the Balkans it was not confined to any single group. As the Bulgarian ethnologist Mikhail Arnaudov wrote in his survey of Balkan rainmaking ceremonies and songs:

> In name as well as in essence, here we do have a pan-Balkan ritual. The resemblances that indicate such a unity are spread through all elements of the dances, beliefs and spells. [...] With some small variations, everything here points to a single basic type, known equally among all Balkan peoples.
>
> To pose questions about where the ritual sprang up, or what forms it took elsewhere within the large yet relatively closed cultural and historical area occupied by Balkan people, seems almost inappropriate. Not only are the rudiments lost in the remote past but the [. . .] equalising influences deprive us of any grounds for firm hypotheses.[3]

2. Ivanov and Toporov use the term "typologically parallel". See note 4 below.
3. Arnaudov, Mikhail, *Studii vurhu bulgariskite obredi i legendi* [*Studies on Bulgarian Customs and Legends*], Bulgarian Academy of Sciences, Sofia: 1924 edition, pp. 247-302; and 1971 edition, vol 1, pp. 155-201. Extract tr. Anelia Tapp & RB.

So it seems impossible to trace the ritual's precise lines of development. Yet, despite Arnaudov's commendable reticence in ascribing theories of origin, other scholars appear to agree that it was first practised among Slavic (or possibly Balto-Slavic or proto-Slavic) tribes, and then disseminated to other groups. Even so, since there is no archaeological evidence and a complete absence of artefacts of any kind as far as the rainmaking ceremonies themselves are concerned, and since the first written records about them date only from the early nineteenth century, the best clues available for any kind of historical reconstruction are reports and, more recently, interviews and recordings from travellers, ethnographers and other witnesses and observers, supported by whatever circumstantial evidence may be gleaned – or reconstituted – from comparative linguistics and mythology.

Even though it is clear that all such reconstructions can only be regarded as tentative, they do offer us some clues which amount to more than pure fancy or guesswork. Various scholars have traced fascinating similarities and correspondences between the Balkan ceremonies and far more ancient religious rituals, so that some tantalisingly appealing, attractive and plausible theories have been put forward, all indicating that the names given to the participants in these Balkan ceremonies are likely to reflect archaic mythological motifs and personages. For example, one group of names for the rain-maiden, of the type *Peperuda*, probably links with the name of the Slavonic thunder god, *Perun*, and/or his Baltic equivalent *Perkunas*; and this may apply to the other names too.[4] Comparative linguists and mythologists have also traced further possible connections with myths associated with rain in ancient India, especially via the *Rig Veda*; not to mention with names of Hittite, Lithuanian, Icelandic, Etruscan, Roman and Greek figures. Some scholars have postulated reconstruction of the origins of the rituals to as far back as the Neolithic period.[5]

Perhaps rather obviously, the customs are readily interpretable as a branch or scion of seasonal fertility rites. Dražen Nožinić writes:

> The peoples of south-east Europe have until recent times known various customs and magical rituals by means of which they have attempted to influence atmospheric phenomena, i.e. to maintain a balance in nature, particularly

4. This theory was proposed by Roman Jakobson. See: 'Slavic Gods and Demons' (1958) and 'Linguistic Evidence in Comparative Mythology' (1964), *Selected Writings*, Vol. VII, pp. 6-7 & 22-3.
5. Apart from Arnaudov and Jakobson, other interesting and original contributors to theories of ancient antecedents include: Skok, Petar: *Etimologiski rječnik hrvtatskoga ili srpskoga jezika* [*Etymological Dictionary of the Croatian or Serbian Language*], 1973, Vol. 3, pp. 55-6 & 603; and Ivanov, V. V. & Toporov, V. I.: *Issledovanya v oblasti slavyanskih drevnotstei* [*Researches in the Field of Slavonic Antiquities/Folklore*], Moscow, 1974, pp. 104 ff.

in times when there was a threat of drought. It is believed that these customs were born in the Neolithic period, and they have been noted in ethnographic literature in various parts of the world. As far as the Balkan Slavs are concerned, it is not hard to differentiate these customs from those which are performed at particular times of the year. Even so, both these categories possess many common features which suggest far more aspects in common than any indications of external similarities to the forms of either type of enactment taken singly. Throughout the literature, the emphasis has been on the similarities between south-Slavic rainmaking customs and the rural customs which belong to the spring-summer cycle. So, on the basis of these facts, the rainmaking customs may be considered as a sub-group within the wider category of customs which aim to ensure fertility.[6]

*

Despite the enormous and fascinating variations to be found in details of the rainmaking rituals throughout the Balkans (and not just from region to region but sometimes from one village to the next), the underlying unity among them seems incontrovertible. Nor were they confined to one religious group: in Kosovo, as elsewhere, they were practised by both Christians and Moslems. The leading rain-maiden has been variously described as being from a poor and humble family, as a pauper, an orphan, a non-privileged person and as the youngest daughter of a widow who never remarried and was past childbearing age. There is general emphasis on her lowliness, modesty and purity; and she always went barefoot, perhaps to emphasise her humility or, rather, humbleness and, more simply, her direct connection with the soil. In this way, it might be said, she was "earthed".

In many areas, the role passed gradually to the Romas, till they took it up exclusively. In certain areas, to be a rain-maiden even became a seasonal profession for Roma girls and young women, which involved them in travelling around to perform the ceremonies for various village communities. It is unclear whether they confined themselves to areas in which their families regularly moved, or went further afield. Far more detailed work needs to be done, and done quickly, in researching the role of the Roma in carrying on the tradition. It may soon be altogether too late to discover anything at all about this.

6. Nožinić, Dražen: 'Postupci za prizivanje kiše na Kordunu, Banija i Moslavini' ['Rainmaking Rituals in Kordun, Banija and Moslavina'], *Raskovnik*, No. 91-92, Belgrade, 1998, pp. 75 ff. Extract tr. Vera Radojević & RB.

The custom diminished in scale and importance throughout the nineteenth and twentieth centuries, partly because of official disapproval and at times outright censorship, first on the part of the church and later by communist authorities, both of whose proponents and administrators deemed such practices improper, immoral, primitive or degenerate. Rulers, it seems, tend to be prudes regardless of their ideologies.

*

So far as I have been able to discover, the first person ever to report, document and transcribe the rainmaking songs and ceremonies was the Serbian collector, language reformer, dictionary-compiler and translator, Vuk Stefanović Karadžić (1787-1864).

He included an entry on "Dodola" in the first edition of his *Srpski Rjecnik* (*Serbian Dictionary*), published in Vienna in 1815. Through subsequent editions of the *Dictionary* (1857), the first volume of his collection *Srpske narodne pjesme* (*Folk Songs of the Serbian People*, 1841) and his posthumously published study *Život i običaji naroda srpskoga* (*Life and Customs of the Serbian People, 1867*), the rainmaking customs and songs became well-known to such internationally renowned poets and scholars as Goethe – whom Karadžić himself met.

While Karadžić consistently uses the word *djevojke* ("girls"), an English traveller to Serbia in the 1840s, Alexander Paton, took pains to point out that the leading participant was by no means a mere-slip-of-a-girl:

> One of the most extraordinary customs of Servia is that of the Dodola. When a long drought has taken place, a handsome young woman is stripped, and so dressed up with grass, flowers, cabbage and other leaves, that her face is scarcely

visible; she then, in company with several girls of twelve to fifteen years of age, goes from house to house singing a song, the burden of which is a wish for rain. It is then the custom of the mistress of the house at which the Dodola is stopped to throw a little water on her.[7]

Following Karadžić, Paton adds, "This custom used also to be kept up in the Servian districts of Hungary, but has been forbidden by the priests."

The Serbian writer Dimitrije Nikolajević told me, in Belgrade in October 2000, that in his childhood, in rural areas near Kragujevac, villagers deliberately set out to choose "the most beautiful girls, aged sixteen or seventeen, for the roles of *dodolas*." Another Serbian writer, Mila Bosić, says that in the village of Banatske Here in Vojvodina, "the *dodola*, who was a gypsy, had to be pregnant."[8] Dražen Nožinić, a particularly thorough researcher, writes:

This work is based on the results of the author's own fieldwork between 1989 and 1991 in two hundred and ninety villages in Kordun, Banija and Moslavina as well as in the surrounding areas[...]. The period of time for which the details were collected covers approximately one hundred years (1870–1970). Thus all the informants interviewed during the course of this research had actually already participated actively in the customs discussed[...]. A few of them were born towards the end of the nineteenth century, and the majority at the beginning of the twentieth century. The youngest were born in the 1920s. The performers were trained and taught by older women, born some 45 to 50 years before the performers themselves. These older women thus transferred their knowledge of traditions in which they themselves had participated. These facts about invoking rain take us back to the last quarter of the nineteenth century. Moreover, certain rites could be and were permitted to be performed only by elderly women, and in this context the 'teachers' appear in a different role, i.e. the informants had themselves participated throughout the whole of their lives in various rites to summon rain. Their fellow villagers, whom they had taught, went on

7. Paton, Archibald: *Servia, The Youngest Member of the European Family, or, A Residence in Belgrade, and Travels in the Highlands and Woodlands of the Interior, during the Years 1843 and 1844*, Longman, Brown, Green and Longmans, London, 1845, pp. 270-271.
8. Bosić, Mila: *Godišnji običaji Srba u Vojvodini* [*Annual Customs of Serbs in Vojvodina*], Novi Sad & Sremska Mitrovica, 1996, pp. 341-345.

performing these rites right up to the 1980s, when most of the rituals were eventually given up. [9]

This passage not only provides insights into the survival of the rite and the ages of participants but implies that, in many villages, "inner" knowledge of rainmaking rituals was an integral part of female "magical" lore, and passed on either in matrilineal fashion or at least solely among women. It is a pity that we have no authoritative reports by female ethnographers who have been allowed in on these preparatory rituals. It is tempting to interpret Nožinić's information in terms of a genuine "mystery" and, what is more, to perceive the rite as a descendant of far more ancient female fertility ceremonies. [10]

*

On the age of participants, then, there exists considerable difference of opinion, which certainly reflects a wide variety of divergent practices. Some commentators say that the ages of the girls gradually diminished from between around eleven and sixteen to between five and ten years; and others, usually envisioning or interpreting the ceremony in terms of a specific *rite de passage* from childhood to readiness for sexual activity, argue that crucial criteria for the selection of the rain-maiden were prepubescence, and/or virginity/chastity.

While these are certainly oversimplifications which in any case do not

9. Nožinić, Dražen: 'Postupci za prizivanje kiše na Kordunu, Banija i Moslavini' ['Rainmaking Rituals in Kordun, Banija and Moslavina'], *Raskovnik*, No. 91-92, Belgrade, 1998, pp. 76-7. Extract tr. Vera Radojević & RB.

10. Perhaps such as those enacted and performed at Eleusis? A question to be left, for the time being at least and perhaps forever, dangling. But a question mooted by several scholars, most notably, by Ivanov & Toporov, op. cit., in suggesting an etymological connection between the name of the rainmaking celebrant in Dalmatia, *Prporuše*, and the goddess Persephone.

fit all the facts, there is little doubt that a specifically childlike naivety does appear through all the recorded rain-maidens' songs, which are recognisably distinct in tone from other genres of folksongs performed by adults in the same geographical areas. It seems at least possible, then, that the rites had always involved young girls, at least as members of the leading rain-maiden's troupe, in much the same way as they may well have done in Minoan and Mycenaean religious ceremonies.[11] It is also apparent that the rain-maiden's intimate association with the *pouring* of fresh water in itself provides the clearest possible indication of her "purity".[12] Whatever her age, the key factor is not only that she "stands on a threshold", but that she herself represents or embodies it. As the Bulgarian anthropologist Florentina Badalanova pointed out to me in London in 2000, in every respect her necessary condition is "liminal".

*

It perhaps also needs to be added here that, by comparison with some of the narrative epics or love songs in the various Balkan traditions, the rainmaking songs in general can hardly be described as masterpieces of oral literature.[13] In their simplicity of style, their "naive" and "intimate" vocabulary and their obvious, unsophisticated rhymes, many of these songs are reminiscent of children's jingles all over the world. Shortly before his death in 2000, E. D. Goy, the last teacher of Serbo-Croatian language and literature at Cambridge University, told me that the Balkan rainmaking songs reminded him of children's jingles in the British Isles. He quoted a Welsh song which he remembered from his own childhood:

> A soul cake, a soul cake, a soul cake,
> Please, Good Missus, a soul cake –
>
> An apple, a pear, a plum or a cherry,
> Any good thing to make us all merry –

11. At least, that is, if we are to accept the interpretations from seals and similar artefacts offered by Sir Arthur Evans: see 'The Ring of Nestor', *The Journal of Hellenic Studies*, 1925, vol. XLV, London, 1925, pp. 1-75.

12. See, for example, Djordjević, M.: *Život i običaji narodni u Leskovačkoj Moravi*, [*Life and Folk Customs Around Leskovac on the River Morava*], Belgrade, 1901, reprinted by the Serbian Academy of Sciences, Belgrade, 1955, 1958, pp. 401-403.

13. Such as the Serbian oral epic ballads, as translated by Geoffrey Locke (*The Serbian Epic Ballads*, Nolit, Belgrade, 1997; Association of Serbian Writers Abroad, London, 2002) and by many others; and recorded and studied by Milman Parry and A. B. Lord (Lord, A. B.: *The Singer of Tales*, Harvard, 1960).

One for Peter, two for Paul,
And three for Him who made us all.

This chant may be compared with some lines in a Dalmatian rainmaking song, sung by boys, youths and unmarried bachelors, quoted by Vuk Stefanović Karadžić:

> Grant us, mistress,
> An oke of flour, mistress,
> A fleecelet of wool, mistress,
> A portion of cheese, mistress,
> A handful of salt, mistress,
> Two or three eggs, mistress,
> God be with you, mistress,
> For you have bestowed gifts upon us.[14]

14. *Život i običaji naroda srpskoga* [*Life and Customs of the Serbian People*], 1867, reprinted in *Vukove Zapisi* [*Vuk's notes*], Srpksa književna zadruga [Serbian Literary Co-operative], Belgrade, 1957. p. 65. Extract tr. Vera Radojević & RB.

Richard Burns's latest book, *In a Time of Drought* (Shoestring Press), is a seven-part poem-sequence about the fall of Yugoslavia. It is based in part on the material he writes about here and it contains further notes and a glossary on the Balkan rainmaking customs.

The four photographs accompanying this essay, which depict two *dodolas* in the village of Banja Koviljaca, near Loznica in Western Serbia, were taken in 1957 by a Dr. Dragić. The photographs are reproduced here with the kind permission of the National Ethnographic Museum, Belgrade, where they form part of the Serbian National Ethnographic Archive.

A Wild Goose Speaks To Me

YANG LIAN

"There is no international, only different locals": my essay 'The International inside the Local' is summed up by this statement. What is "local"? Are its contents geographical, psychological, historical, based on language or even linguistics? How can a poet write a poem entitled 'The archaeology of the now'? The poet archaeologist, as if uncovering layer upon layer of earth, seeks the ever more deeply-hidden self; and the poem, like an archaeological manual, records the experience of excavating ever deeper within one site. And for us, the depth we reach through the process of comparing poem with poem (especially with a poet's earlier work) confirms the value and the status of that poem, to the point that "local" doesn't at all signify a specific site, but must point to all sites, as being the ability of the poet to excavate his own self. The poet says, "Give me a single breath, and I will grow roots, penetrate the soil, probe shingle and magma, and hear the sea through every artery and vein of groundwater, sharing the voyage of every navigator since the dawn of time".

So on this summer night, through the open window of my bedroom, direct to my eardrum, comes the cry of a wild goose, shattering the dark green glassy silence of London, and in the timbre of every chilly honk a secret world is uncovered. What I want to know is, what is it that's touching my heart so much?

Is it this city of London? It's one of countless foreign towns I've drifted through. Originally, as with other temporary resting places, the Stoke Newington postcode, still unmemorised, then discarded, shrunken, fixed and buried in my CV, became just a line of letters no-one paid any attention to. But against all expectation I went on living there. Some years after the city had become gradually familiar; as "of their own accord" my eyes began to look for the last apple on the branches of the same apple tree each November. I suddenly realised that my relationship with London had changed. We no longer rubbed shoulders as it passed me by, but it had come to a halt, to turn into the first "local" I had had since I left China. Even stranger than simple peripatetic exile, this superficial standstill doubly demonstrated life cannot help but move.

Was it through writing the collection *Lee Valley Poems* in London? These external places are converted into my inner self, to become part of the "I" of the text. In fact, even the word "exile" is empty: if it weren't for the substance of poetry, we wouldn't even be worthy of our own experience. The "blood-dripping funnel" image, which I had to create, comes to include the garden I look down on from my kitchen window as well as all the gardens that sink deep in the autumn rain. The line "confirming the wind also goes away along itself", which I had to find, comes to express the street before us, blown with dry fallen leaves, as well as all the streets the wanderer's road has followed. As the psychological roll-over of time is folded into geographical space, these images become more local the more they point to the theme of human "placelessness". Apart from a line of poetry, we have nowhere to exist.

Or again, are China and Chinese language what the cry of the wild goose summons? At present, I jokingly called them "my own foreign country" and "my foreign mother-tongue". Since long ago, fleeing from home has been seen in China as the cruelest experience that anyone could undergo (and please note that the expression "flee from home" literally translates as "turning your back on the old well [of home]"); so the wild goose that follows the seasons north and south as it migrates become the emblem of the homeless wanderer. Those skeins of geese which form the Chinese character 人 [person] are always going home. Yet the sight-lines of those who watch them fly away can never return home. Skimming through the ancient poetry of the Tang dynasty [618-960 AD], we see the wild goose as practically synonymous with heartbreak and longing. Witness lines such as these: "Returning, wild geese enter an alien sky", or "When the wild geese return they bring many letters from home" by Wang Wei [701-761 AD]; "When the wild goose is lost in blue sky" or "The wild geese guide the sorrowful heart to far away" by Li Bai [701-762 AD]; "The heart flies into extinction with the wild geese" or "Leaves fall as the wild geese go south" by Meng Haoran [689-740 AD]; "On the autumn frontier the wild goose cries once" or "When will the wild geese bring a letter?" by Du Fu [712-770 AD]. Du Fu, who was by far the most adept at describing the hardships of the wandering life, has a poem simply titled 'A Solitary Wild Goose', which contains the couplet "Who pities a shard of shadows / lost to each other inside many-layered clouds?": long ago, he set down a definitive description of the situation I which I find myself today.

Classical Chinese poetry emphasises allusion, which, by means of "inter-modularity", allows all tradition to be contained in a newly-written text. At the instant of hearing the cry of the wild goose I am drawn into the Tang dynasty, making Lee Valley's waters flow twelve hundred years upstream – and isn't that a kind of "distance" or actually, a "nearness" pressing toward to me? I could almost greet all the Du Fu's as they hurry past the corner of the street huddled in their long scholars' gowns, just as I greet my well-known and familiar neighbours.

Poetry includes all of that. Here "distant" and "deep" mean the same thing. The poet may travel far, but never really leave the autochthonous ground of his own inner self. The world slips by him like an abstract setting, and the distance between its fluctuating changes exists only in the direction of the internal inquiry. The poet's standards shift as the poetry imperceptibly moves towards the vertical. That is to say, so-called "depth" solely indicates the poet's comprehension of existence, as seen in his writing: Heidegger's statement that "All great thinkers have spoken the same thought" is pointing out this idea about "existence". The value and the joy of poetry can be described as fishing in the deep sea of existence. In comparison with the substance of this, the pursuit of changes in subject matter, novelty of form, individuality of style, even political correctness or identity games – these are all shadows, aims which are too superficial and which will weaken the meaning of the poetry. Sticking with "the human condition", a poem contains a definite set of concentric circles: Tang poetry, China, foreign countries, London, the Lee Valley, my tiny study, the specific moment of writing a word, the non-time implied by the tenselessness characteristic of the Chinese verb, these are all in the "I". When they are no longer merely knowledge, but have become the poet's "thought", then a poem has connected with the energy source of itself.

I know that today, when the post-modern is so pervasive, there are dangers in discussing or even raising the issue of "depth". But today's reality is tense, full of the smell of gunpowder even more than was the Cold War. Today's art theory has been able to stand before the sediment of the twentieth century and reflect on its superstitious faith in novelty of from. Today's philosophical question – the precise antonym for "today'" – is just this: how can we abolish the mirage of time, and face anew the emptiness and darkness which have been eternally co-existent with human nature? In a word, the energy to do so comes from the awareness of the predicament. If an inopportune or out-of-style idea can continue to create good poetry, then that is the nature of poetry.

I didn't know the wild goose that cried to me on that summer night, but I have heard in it the skeins of wild geese that have flown over every poet in every era, and they have never migrated from that clear and melodic voice.

Yang Lian's poem 'The Journey', on which this essay reflects, is printed on pp 22-4.

Priora

KITTY SULLIVAN

Poetry and photography share much common ground. A great deal of the best poetry being written today is filmic and a single line, if written well, should be able to draw the reader to it in a way not dissimilar to that of a good photograph. However, poetry and photography do not always combine well artistically; various collections have shown this over recent years. The initiative has to be a novel one.

Priora provides a new focus on the importance of objects to specific poems or to a poet's own writing practice. Fifty leading UK poets are asked to choose an object that follows these guiding principles. All photographs are shot with a narrow depth of field (f-stop 4) which shows an object in focus and the poet out of focus; thus removing the notion of celebrity. Poems written about these objects correspond to the photographs. The project relies on a coherence of narrative between the poet, object and photograph.

By the time this short introduction goes to press, over half the featured poets will have been photographed for the project; the selection in this issue of *Poetry Review* being the first time these photographs have been seen. Midway through our cast-list of poets and what is apparent is that the objects that poets have decided upon seem gender-specific. Male poets (to be featured in a later issue of *Poetry Review*) have frequently selected robust, disposable objects, knives or bullets. Conversely, female poets have tended to opt for more organic objects, curvilinear in form, which relate to display or domesticity.

On completion, *Priora* (which is sponsored by Metro Imaging) will be exhibited at art galleries nationally. Plans are under way to have an anthology edited by John Burnside and James Byrne of all fifty UK poets, by early 2007.

❧

Kitty Sullivan has emerged as one of London's finest young photographers. She is a graduate from The Byam Shaw School of Art and was shortlisted for the 'Addictions' project as part of the Young Photographer's competition in 2001. Her work is currently on display at The Glass House Gallery. Further exhibitions in 2006 include The Hackwood Art Festival, Norwich Fringe Festival and The Place Theatre. She works as a portrait photographer for SomaPhotos.com and designs *The Wolf* poetry magazine.

Pascale Petit

Sasha Dugdale

Eva Salzman

Ruth Padel

Mimi Khalvati

Ruth Fainlight

POETIC LICENSE

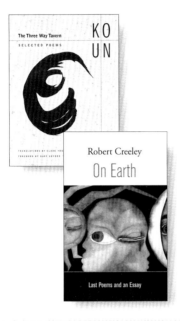

On Earth
Last Poems and an Essay
ROBERT CREELEY

"*On Earth* provides a kind of closure on a rich poetic life and brings us intimately in contact with the poet's final thoughts on the great themes of time and memory."
—**Michael Davidson**

£13.95 cloth

The Three Way Tavern
Selected Poems
KO UN
Foreword by Gary Snyder
Translations by Clare You and Richard Silberg

"Ko Un is a crucial poet for the twenty-first century and this is an enormously fresh and vivid translation."
—**Robert Hass**

£10.95 paper

New in the New California Poetry Series

The Wilds
MARK LEVINE

In his third book of poems, Levine continues his exploration of the rhythms and forms of memory. Austere and lyrical, the music of these poems resonates with echoes of poetic tradition yet is singularly modern.
£10.95 paper

The Totality for Kids
JOSHUA CLOVER

"Fierce intelligence, fierce understanding of social issues, and fierce sense of the power of artifice. This is major work, haunted by a sense of totality always present in the formal intricacy and in the roles cities and architecture play."
—**Charles Altieri, author of**
The Art of Twentieth-Century American Poetry
£10.95 paper

I Love Artists
New and Selected Poems
MEI-MEI BERSSENBRUGGE

Drawing on four decades of work and including new poems published here for the first time, this selection of Berssenbrugge's poetry displays the extraordinary luminosity characteristic of her style—its delicate, meticulous observation, great scenic imagination, and unusual degree of comfort with states of indetermination, contingency, and flux.
£12.95 paper

At booksellers or (44) (1243) 842165 • www.ucpress.edu

 UNIVERSITY OF CALIFORNIA PRESS

REVIEWS

Is the mastery of the long line shown by American poets, in part, a gift from Ireland?
—Alison Brackenbury

Language's Mercury

DAVID MORLEY

Rapture, Carol Ann Duffy, Picador, £12.99, ISBN 0330412809;
Chaotic Angels: Poems in English, Gwyneth Lewis,
Bloodaxe, £9.95, ISBN 1852247231

Fluency is rapture, Virginia Woolf claimed. Momentum in writing is like a perpetual motion machine, issuing words on words. Without impulsion, the enterprise becomes a trudge; surprises grow rare or prefabricated. Writers operate on the same artistic plane for a time, working through several pieces of writing or even several books. However, given sufficient fluency through practice, they make artistic breakthroughs and leaps while writing one particular piece; a poem or short story, say. Carol Ann Duffy's *Rapture* is such a breakthrough: one story; one feat of fluency; extreme momentum in the telling. It flows free of her previous work, and that of her contemporaries. She is not writing for other poets; she has slipped out of their rulebook.

Even the cover calls for judgement: inflamed red boards, and a gilt illustration of Duffy's leitmotifs: a moon, shooting stars, an astounded figure with arms upraised. It feels like childhood literature; it looks unharmed, unwarned. The book's very strangeness starts there, and with its poems' taut titles tipped down the contents page in a strip. Yet the poems are a kind of anti-literature, apparently simple, reading at times as if they were someone's first poems, so stripped, so plain, so open to objection and self-objection, that they enact the story of the book: the birth, life, death, and afterlife of love: the aloneness of it. Her keynote is simplicity of voice, but that does not mean this work is simplistic:

> Then the birds stitching the dawn with their song
> have patterned your name.
>
> Then the green bowl of the garden filling with light
> is your gaze.
>
> Then the lawn lengthening and warming itself
> is your skin.

Then a cloud disclosing itself overhead
is your opening hand.

'Absence'

Simplicity is a hard melt for a writer: the etymologies of words are anecdotes told by language across time. Words prickle with meanings; but they are slippery with their histories and usages. Duffy knows this inside out; that language is mercury. She also knows that sliding her archetype-nouns towards a reader – moon, love, world, rose, kiss, star, time – draws an audience to their familiar shapes. However, making simplicity inevitable is a matter of nerve and rewriting. Allowing these open-hearted poems to ride on their melting is therefore very daring. This is probably the best thing of its kind since Douglas Dunn's *Elegies*, which it often echoes in the stamina and grace of its diction.

What is especially interesting is that this book is, as it were, written out of humiliation; and yet the whole project is utterly cunning. The architecture of the arrangement; the literary weighing up in 'The Love Poem'; the self-conscious allusions to and collusions with *The Rubaiyat, The Song of Solomon,* even *Sonnets from the Portuguese*: this is deliberated anguish – articulated, transformed, and tested. By stripping her art form to its elements, Duffy is reinventing an audience for her poetry: the kind of audience that accepts and longs for a poetry whose purpose is partly moral instruction.

We must allow the fact that poetry does not feature in some people's lives. That does not mean we cold-shoulder them. If they choose not to go to poetry, then we might do something to open poetry to them. Duffy has created an open space for many readers who might not come to it otherwise. What this book permits you to see is the visible head of an iceberg, with Duffy's lovers frozen inside it, locked and alive. What she hides extremely well is the knowledge and work submerged hugely beneath this structure. So, while *Rapture* deserves much applause for its emotional honesty, consolation, and generosity, it also deserves praise for its cunning, its impersonality, and its mercilessness, all of which virtues make the invisible work of poetry an act of concentrated ferocity.

Watching the levels of artistic growth in Gwyneth Lewis's work has been a delight; *Chaotic Angels* is a display of this momentum. Only George Szirtes rivals her in the fluency and humanity with which she handles forms and poem sequences. Like Szirtes, she is a linguistic virtuoso: she is the first writer to be awarded the Welsh laureateship. However, this book brings together poems from three collections in English. Those collections –

beginning in 1995 with *Parables and Faxes* – performed the hat-trick of being total books, not portfolios of individual pieces.

All her books employ an implicit architecture; you might say Gwyneth Lewis uses a book as a long poetic form. This architecture becomes more explicit in *Zero Gravity* and *Keeping Mum* as she maintains focus on a particular subject, as a novelist would or a maker of creative nonfiction.

However, her increasing micro-organisation of form and of various restrictive practices creates amazing tectonic shifts of voice and syntax, none of which holds up the progress of any book, and all of which feel as inevitable as a well-made story. It is interesting that Lewis has written (and written very well) books of creative non-fiction. One practice feeds another, generously. Her poetry in Welsh is, to my mind, as powerful as her work in English. One language flows on another: water on water, not oil and water. Her poetry never feels like some hybrid of worldly reality and its translation into the supreme fiction, nor is it a game of language where the play is everything and the poetry some second thought. In her way, Gwyneth Lewis is as cunning and generous as the angel who states that, "Every disease is a work of art / if you play it rightly":

> By this he meant: whatever the form
> imposed by arthritis, or by the gout.
> your job's to compose yourself round about
> its formal restrictions, and make that sing,
> even to death. […]

> 'Angel of Healing'

David Morley's next collection of poetry is *The Invisible Kings* (Carcanet Press, 2007).

Unquiet Landscapes

MATTHEW JARVIS

John Kinsella, *The New Arcadia: Poems*, Norton, $27.95, ISBN 0393060535;
John Kinsella, *Peripheral Light: Selected and New Poems*, selected and with
an introduction by Harold Bloom, Norton, $14.95, ISBN 0393327051

In these two volumes, both of which are rooted in his native Western Australia, John Kinsella shows himself to be a landscape poet of considerable sophistication. The word 'landscape' is chosen advisedly here. Kinsella himself has written that "Landscape is the appropriate word for me, as it's about human mediation of the environment". In other words, there is no sense that Kinsella feels he is simply recording the land over which his poetry travels; instead, the linguistic act "becomes its own place" (as he has put it). Or, in slightly different terms, Kinsella's landscape poetry functions very definitely as a discursive patterning of the land he writes.

Kinsella's poetry thus creates its own mythical map of the Western Australian wheatbelt on which it is primarily focused, with certain locations gaining crucial geo-poetic significance. For example, each of the five Acts into which *The New Arcadia* is divided begins with a 'Drive' – literally, a drive in the car across the Western Australian landscape:

> This is the drive to York,
> repetition, imprint of incursion
> and memory, unwinding daily.

The five 'Drives' form a geographical spine to *The New Arcadia* as a whole – the same road, travelled at different times, offering a primary space out of which a broader understanding of the speaker's locale emerges. Thus, it is on the road that we first encounter Mount Bakewell, a psychological centre-point for Kinsella's persona:

> Heading back, going home, it's the sight
> of Mount Bakewell that acts chemically,
> the fluctuation of serotonin levels,
> […] the mountain hidden,
> but you know it's there: compulsive,
> creating weather, full of contradictions.

Similarly, the road is a place that reveals human interactions with the landscape: the "trucks accelerating to test out / their roo bars", "An old commune: / sheds, smashed asbestos sheeting", and the scattering of rubbish ("Plastic containers linger, a few / hubcaps spinning off"). Moreover, the road also becomes a space out of which more general meditations on the land and its people emerge, as the speaker considers topics as divergent as the progress of salt, Australian masculinity, and relationships with Aboriginal culture. Kinsella's road is, in effect, a generative locale out of which broader landscapes can emerge, through both observation and contemplation.

As each Act of *The New Arcadia* starts with a 'Drive', so each ends with an eclogue. The potential for interaction which the eclogue's dialogue form offers helps Kinsella's dramatic capacity to emerge, thus creating an effective contrast to the more contemplative 'Drives'. Indeed, the dramatic mode pushes Kinsella into a particular sharpness of vision, which is perhaps in danger of being obscured in some of his more discursive, meditative pieces. In addition to the five Act-concluding eclogues, the middle of Act 3 offers one more – one that is, significantly, set right in the middle of the volume as a whole. This is the superb 'Eclogue of Presence', which pits a farmer against a 'Young Bloke'. The publisher's flyer for the collection suggests that the farmer "defiantly rebukes a local youth for his romantic notions". However, this is an unfortunate simplification of what is a far more complex piece. On one level, the puncturing of romance is undoubtedly true: the farmer observes unflinchingly that "the bat sounds and nightjar noise / are quelled by rifle and chainsaw". But this is also a poem about history. The apparently Aboriginal 'Young Bloke' is conscious of the way in which the farmer's "family brought mourning / to my cousins". He is also highly critical of the farmer's *wadjela* (non-Aboriginal) lifestyle, associating him with killing and choking natural phenomena, and accusing him of profound environmental ignorance:

> You don't even know the names of evening
> or the character of bones that give substance to the hills,
> and the stories of even the brightest morning
> are hidden from you, unna?

Kinsella's capturing of both social and historical conflict in this central piece is superbly managed, and is neatly suggestive of the dramas to which the wheatbelt is home.

Between the 'Drives' and the eclogues, *The New Arcadia* offers a variety of other (frequently shorter) pieces, many of which are meditations on the diverse life of the area. For example, Act 1 contains poems about snakes

('Warning – Snakes (Reprise)') and bats ('They Say of Bats…'), alongside a piece which invokes the gossipy interactions of a whole town ('The Telephone Paddock'). Similarly, Act 2 presents a poem about roadkill ('Roadkill Shock Rocks the Galah's World…') alongside one about townspeople who are culling birds which "sing / Too loud" ('The Cull'). Such pieces are typically strong in themselves; but they crucially build up as the collection progresses so that the characters and locations which Kinsella develops over two hundred pages suggest a literary geography potentially as rich as William Faulkner's Yoknapatawpha County.

Peripheral Light is a very useful introduction to Kinsella's work – although original publication dates on the selected poetry would have helped the reader track poetic development. Crucially, it makes clear one more point that demands emphasis. This is simply that much of Kinsella's material is resolutely anti-pastoral. *The New Arcadia* is the more developed of the two books in terms of its engagement with land and its creatures. However, it is still obviously a working-through of the particular landscape discourse that is apparent from the very start of *Peripheral Light* – a discourse which is characterised by a conviction that the landscapes of rural Western Australia are, in various ways, significantly blighted. Thus, 'Pillars of Salt' observes:

> the roads
> sinking, the soil weeping (scab on scab
> lifted), fences sunk to gullies
> catching the garbage of paddocks.

Similarly, 'The Myth of the Grave' suggests that the very earth is unquiet here:

> The ground dries and crumbles,
> a lizard darts out of a crack
> and races across the paddock.
> Do ashes rest easily here?

These two collections definitely repay careful reading. Kinsella is not always an easy poet, and certain pieces are decidedly difficult (for example, the seven 'essays' on 'Linguistic Disobedience' in *Peripheral Light*). However, such difficulties are rarely unalleviated, and what Kinsella typically offers is a highly effective combination of densely interwoven linguistic detail and moments of relative simplicity. Thus, a poem such as 'The Shitheads of Spray' (*The New Arcadia*, Act 3) sets linguistic richness ("Under-ode, antediluvian reprisal, / seed vengeance, broad-leaf outrage"; "Spray-drift sensurround, surround sounds / but furtively sibilant, odour-ploy") alongside the very straightforward:

> the shitheads of spray
> graze sheep on dying grass
> and smile benignly.

Kinsella's poetic power is often in precisely this combination, and in the sense that – through a complex accretion of observations and meditations – his poetry is a mature fulfilment of Jonathan Bate's call, in *The Song of the Earth*, for a "song that names the earth", for a poetry which serves as a reminder that "it is we who have the power to determine whether the earth will sing or be silent". In short, these two collections – and *The New Arcadia* in particular – suggest the coming to full maturity of an extremely important poet. Or, to put it even more plainly, this is work that deserves to be very widely read.

Matthew Jarvis is currently writing a book called *Place and Environment in Radical British Poetry* (for Rodopi).

ℬ

I Think Alone

STEVEN MATTHEWS

Lynette Roberts, *Collected Poems*, edited by Patrick McGuinness, Carcanet, £12.95, ISBN 1857548426

Perhaps the most surprising thing about this *Collected Poems* is that, in many senses, it presents the work of an occasional poet. Virtually all of the work included here was written within a single decade of Roberts's eighty-six year long life. Since that period of intense writing stretches from the early 1940s, the occasion of many of the poems – even when seemingly pastoral or love lyric – is the ground bass of loss and violence which can suddenly devastatingly erupt into ordinary local lives. Roberts was a unique figure, a Welsh poet who was born and lived her young childhood in Argentina. It is only in her 'South American' lyrics that the immediate shadow of the contemporary war is lifted. At this partly-imagined, partly-recalled remove, the celebration of nature can be unreserved, if never without unexpected purpose, as in these lines of stark contrast at the end of 'Royal Mail':

> Outside sweating gourds
> Dripping rind and peel; yet inside cool as lemon,
> Orange, avocado pear.
> While in this damp and stony stare of a village
> Such images are unknown:
> So would I think upon these things
> In the event that someday I shall return to my native surf
> And feel again the urgency of sun and soil.

The yearning for urgency is typical, and releases the energies in many of the lyrics in the first part of this book. Roberts is a strikingly ambitious poet, given the brevity of her writing life; ambitious in her use of form to enhance the vigour of the poetry's speaking voice. This collection contains experiments in Welsh forms alongside Greek metrics, ballads, sonnets, even villanelles. But it is the invigilated restlessness, and concurrent desire for settledness, a kind of impatience with the expressive possibilities of any one form or statement, which create the excitement when reading her work. Even within a single poem, the transitions are abrupt and revelatory. 'The Shadow Remains', one of several poems voicing the plight of the woman left behind by the soldier gone to war, is about the thwarting in these conditions of ability "to speak of everyday things with ease". Instead, the woman must more honestly speak of the shiftlessness of this life, and of the

> [...] brazier fire that burns our sorrow,

> Dries weeping socks above on the rack: that knew
> Two angels pinned on the wall – again two.

The work I have quoted so far comes from the first book gathered in this *Collected*, the small volume *Poems* which appeared under T. S. Eliot's editorship from Faber in 1944. A mini-epic, *Gods With Stainless Ears*, in which war again intervenes disastrously in the relationship of two lovers, appeared in 1951. Eliot then rejected a third collection and that, it seems, was the end of Roberts's poetry. This edition is enlivened by some of the interchange between Roberts and her editor, as it is also by instances from her correspondence with Robert Graves about her work. In both cases, Roberts writes to her lauded male contemporaries as at least an equal: resisting some of Eliot's suggestions for verbal changes in her work and drawing upon some of her comprehensive knowledge of local myth and legend to inform Graves at the time he was working on *The White Goddess.*

When she seeks to include something of that knowledge in her own work, however, the result is disappointing. After learning to relish the lyrics of *Poems*, with their sometimes shocking concatenation of subject ('Lamentation', for instance, includes an odd incident when farm animals were killed in an air raid alongside distress at a miscarriage), *Gods With Stainless Ears* represents a rebarbative experience. Anxious to set her contemporary narrative within recurring cycles, Roberts deploys paradoxically-disruptive syntax and specialist geological or chemical vocabularies. Roberts's own plethora of annotation to each part of *Gods* perhaps leads the editor of this edition, Patrick McGuinness, to claim that her closest poetic peer was David Jones. But Roberts's work seems to me to lack the "key to all mythologies" drive of Jones. She seems, in her askance and community-focused perspective upon wider dynamics, as in her delight in obscure vocabulary, closer to another of the poets sponsored by Eliot at this time, W. S. Graham.

Gods has momentary intensity in its descriptions of the woman left behind, of the conflict between lovers, of the Welsh landscape. But it is in the lyrics of *Poems* and some of the uncollected later work (the 'Green Madrigals', 'Englyn', 'Premonition') that Roberts's distinctive, strange, and wonderful distillation occurs, as in the opening stanza of 'Ecliptic Blue':

> In the cold when sea-mews flake the sky
> With their curmurring fight for the eye
> Of food on water blue, I think of snow.
> I think alone.

Carcanet are to be praised, as on their similarly well-annotated and -introduced edition of George Oppen a few years ago, for their enterprise and courage in making such questioningly modernist writing available again. There is much in Roberts that should be pondered by, and which will prove instructive for, contemporary writers and readers.

Steven Matthews's latest book is *Modernism*, in the Arnold Context Series of which he is General Editor.

B

Fluent Musics

ALISON BRACKENBURY

John F. Deane, *The Instruments of Art*, Carcanet, £8.95, ISBN 1857547861

Lapsed from Protestantism to cheerful paganism, I bring no automatic sympathy to John F. Deane's renderings of a Catholic childhood through *The Instruments of Art*. But the forms of Deane's art are strongly felt and seductive, secure in line, reassuring in rhyme. 'Late October Evening' takes a certain kind of melodious, rhymed lyric almost to perfection. It melts readers' resistance to divisively old-fashioned diction, as Deane's cadences melt across lines, and the dead return "– like a slow galleon under black sail / nearing". The sea that haunts the poem ebbs into the writer's own calm, "the tide brimming, then falling away".

But Deane's work can also divide art from life by sermonising. The kingfisher's flash fades into "the high / Shock of what is beautiful". His art can lack variety; the "small light on the Pilot wireless" glows several times, like an old story from a forgetful relative. Most divisive is his passion for writing about paintings. The sections about art, though careful, can be leaden.

Yet Deane's accounts of his faith achieve a music with "the fluency of water", in long lines which can accommodate the varying movement of animal and man, as in 'Canvas':

> and once a heron passed, like one of those heaving crates
> from an old war.

Is the mastery of the long line shown by American poets, in part, a gift from Ireland? Certainly Deane's early stories of belief are securely weighed and connected to the plants and animals of Achill. "And when they spoke of lilies of the field / I thought of 'flaggers' and of meadowsweet". His ear for birds – "a wren jitters" – is startlingly tender.

Since faith, and poetry, need not divide time, Deane's 'Adagio molto' can flow wittily in a single line, from Mary "passionate and at work" to "the window-cleaner [...] at the twenty-seventh floor". But suffering disrupts his harmonies. At the end of 'In the Teeth of the Wolf', a terrible poem of a painful death, the aggressive rhythms bear no reconciling music. "I refused / belief in You, Creator. Bridegroom. Wolf." Though Christ reappears, to cook fish, before "his / slow disappearance among the shore-line trees", it is a shock to learn that only with death's "astonishing" division "may you have attained / at last, the fluency of water".

So, at that clouded time when the Old Year slides into the New, with long illness and a rain-soaked garden, I read and re-read the music of John Deane: a fine poet for our lives' divided seasons.

Alison Brackenbury's latest collection is *Bricks and Ballads* (Carcanet 2004). She was one of the judges of the 2005 National Poetry Competition.

ℬ

The Actual Matter of Being

HELEN FARISH

Sharon Olds, *Selected Poems*, Cape, £12, ISBN 0224976884

Matter preoccupies the American poet, Sharon Olds. Physical matter, the matter of our bodies. Her belief that "the body on earth is all we have got" means that the body, whether living or dead, female or male, becomes the object of the poet's gaze. And it is the nature of that untiring gaze, the breath-taking precision of the language with which it is given, which most struck me when reading this selection from Olds' seven collections to date. If you are looking for that sense of "adventure in language" which Paul Muldoon described as characterising the best poetry, then this is your book.

"There it was, the actual matter of his being", she writes of the father in 'His Ashes':

> small, speckled lumps of bone
> like eggs; a discoloured curve of bone like a
> fungus grown around a branch,
> spotted pebbles – and the spots were the channels of his marrow
> where the live orbs of the molecules
> swam as if by their own strong will
> and in each cell the chromosomes
> tensed and flashed, tore themselves
> away from themselves, leaving their shining
> duplicates.

The act of opening the urn and the almost scientific gaze on its contents make this poem representative of the kind which some reviewers find inappropriate or even shocking. A review of Olds's 1987 collection, *The Gold Cell*, warned readers they "may be repelled", and rather depressingly a review of this new volume refers to Olds's "repellent candour": "candour" of course reducing the poems from the level of art to mere testimony. Is it repellent to examine the ashes of the father? Should she censor her poetic gaze? Those hostile to her poetic project are of course implicitly arguing that there is a limited range of acceptable subject matter for poetry which Olds transgresses by ignoring the unwritten laws. And significantly she arouses most criticism when female speakers in her poems direct this fierce unshrinking gaze onto their own body. But looking away from the dead, or away from our own living bodies, implies that we are indeed repelled; Olds is asking us not to be, to look closely with her at the matter which comprises our being on this earth. I'm grateful that in 'His Ashes' the speaker was courageous enough to truly look at the "crushed paper-wasp hive" of shards. For me, the gaze both in this poem and across her oeuvre is primarily a deeply compassionate one. Take the close of the poem:

> I looked at him,
> bone and the ash it lay in, chromium-
> white as the shimmering coils of dust
> the earth leaves behind it, as it rolls, you can
> hear its heavy roaring as it rolls away.

The "heavy roaring" of the earth as it "rolls away" tells us all we need to know about the impact of this death on the speaker.

It is "our duty", Olds writes in an early poem, "to find things to love, to bind ourselves to this world." In fact, this *Selected Poems* (1980-2002) reveals to the reader time and again that what Olds finds to bind her to the world is, above all else, language itself. We note in the description of the father's ashes the exactitude, the quest for the precise term, the boiling down of the gaze and then the ambition of its sudden opening out, encompassing the earth itself. In the selection from *Blood, Tin, Straw* (1999), Olds has included two key poems in which the poet reflects on early encounters with language. 'The Prepositions' tells of the "odd comfort" a school girl (previously a 'Behavior Problem') receives from learning a list of prepositions:

> *before, behind, below, beneath,*
> *beside, between,* I stood in that sandstone
> square, and started to tame. *Down,*
> *from, in, into, near,* I was
> located there [.]

"I was / located there" refers to the physical location, the sandstone square, but also crucially to language itself. The apparent innocence of the narration, a girl learning her homework in the playground, gives way to the "breaking of childhood, beginning of memory," the text here highly conscious of its dual function - the prepositions literally placing her and language itself symbolically constructing her identity. The list becomes an "Eden", "*hortus enclosus* where / everything had a place."

Language is also a source of "sharp pleasure" in 'That Day'. A girl refuses to apologise for deliberately spilling ink on her parents' bed and is tied to a chair as punishment. Of the ink, the girl tells us: "I had / felt its midnight, genie shape / leave my chest, pouring forth [...] / and I read that blot. / I read it all day, like a Nancy Drew I was / in." In a much earlier poem, 'Alcatraz', the girl describes her inner badness spreading like ink, but here the spread of ink is associated with empowerment and authority. The text within the text of the poem, the Nancy Drew in which the girl inserts herself as a character, is an example of the kind of framing Olds often engages in and which she uses to bring issues of selfhood and self-consciousness to the fore. When the mother in 'That Day' relents and feeds the girl "hot / alphabet soup", the girl literally consumes language and we can taste her relish:

> I mashed the crescent moon of the C,
> caressed the E, reading with my tongue
> that boiled Braille – and she was almost kneeling to me
> and I wasn't sorry.

Here Olds links writing with the body in the most intimate way; they cannot be disentangled. But neither can the pleasure be disentangled from the pain, for the girl remains tied up whilst being fed the alphabet soup. Under the shelter of an apparently straight forward narrative, this troubling poem explores women's complex relationship with letters.

Poems of childhood, of parenting, bereavement, sexual love, the body: these are Olds' themes, which allow her (as in the poem just discussed) to explore the movements of power. In 'His Ashes', the adult woman opening the urn and sifting through the contents is, on one level, a grieving daughter; but she will also always be the "Eve / [the father] took and pressed back into clay". The act of undoing the urn, therefore, could also be read as an assertion of Eve's power over God the Father. These are without doubt unsettling, challenging poems. But surely we don't want poetry to be a comfortable read.

Helen Farish's *Intimates* won the 2005 Forward Prize for Best First Collection.

Travelling Incognito

DEBJANI CHATTERJEE

Regina Derieva ed. Hildred Crill, *Alien Matter: New and Selected Poems*,
translated by Alan Shaw et al, Spuyten Duyvil, $10.00, ISBN 1933132221;
Knut Ødegard, *Judas Iscariot & Other Poems*, translated by Brian McNeil,
Waxwing (Dublin), £7.95, ISBN 0 954977106;
Pat Boran, *New & Selected Poems*, Salt, £11.99, ISBN 1844711102;
Graham Hartill, *Cennau's Bell: Poems 1980-2001*,
The Collective Press, £8.00, ISBN 1899449019;
Piotr Sommer, *Continued*, translated by Halina Janod et al,
Bloodaxe, £8.95, ISBN 1852247029

Regina Derieva's book contains recent poems from 2002 to 2003 and selections from three previous collections, covering the period 1978 to 2001. Her title, *Alien Matter*, as well as the titles of books from which she has selected – *Absence, The Last War* and *Fugitive* – is revelatory. Hers is a poetry of transition, of exile and often of bitter loss. She has known many changes in her life: born into a Russian Jewish family, she converted to Roman Catholicism, migrated to Israel, had her appeal for Israeli citizenship rejected, and now lives in Sweden. Her translators for *Alien Matter* – Alan Shaw, Robert Reid, Richard McKane, Andrey Gritsman, Peter France, Kevin Carey and Ilya Bernstein – have backgrounds as diverse as the Soviet Union, Britain and the USA.

With its rhyming quatrains, Biblical references, and the focus on country, 'The Land of Ur' is typical of Derieva's poems. The final stanza seems a declaration of her own stateless situation: "It's forbidden. There was a land. / There is no land. One destiny – / now another. And God demands / a sacrificial country." Her poetry brims with the characters and incidents of the Bible, especially the Old Testament. The "wild beasts / of Noah's ark, / which had just devoured / the last dove of peace", the "wide-open eyes" of John the Baptist's severed head, and Lazarus in his coffin, are some of her religious references. Derieva delights in contradictions and is a master of the epigram. 'Maxims and Paradoxes on the Accidental Sheets' begins: "All my life / I sought / an angel. / And he appeared / in order to say: / 'I am no angel!'". Throughout it all she wears her heart on her sleeve – and perhaps this makes her unfashionable among contemporary poets; but hers is a brave and eminently readable voice.

Religion also plays a major role in Norwegian poet Knut Ødegard's *Judas Iscariot & Other Poems*. Ødegard is another convert to Roman

Catholicism and, like many of Derieva's poems, his have the luminous clarity of parables and psalms. Poems like 'Priest' and 'The Farmer' prove his gift for portraying character. 'Uncle Knut' in 'Priest' is quickly sketched as "a practical man, but Latin / was Greek to him" and "more an electrician / than a preacher", a man who literally brings light to his parishioners.

The masterly poem 'Judas Iscariot' tells the Christ story from the point of view of the disciple who betrayed him. A guilt-ridden Judas imagines his own death by hanging – a description that has something of the shock effect of James Kirkup's blasphemous account of the crucified Jesus. Ødegard gets into the mind of the self-righteous disciple who sees his own life and death as paralleling those of Jesus. His obsessive mind links them forever: "For Him I loved – He who betrayed – / I betrayed".

Irishman Pat Boran's *New & Selected Poems* has generous selections from five previous collections as well as eleven new poems. His poems are short narratives of urban life, often set in Dublin, sometimes in London, but always intelligent and humane. Images from daily life are transformed into universal issues of life and death. The haiku, 'A Natural History of Armed Conflict', typical of his quiet and understated short poems, notes war's timeless tragedy: "The wood of the yew / made the bow. And the arrow. / And the grave-side shade". In 'War/Oil' he reminds us that history repeats itself and one ravaged city is like another: "another conflict, another cursed city". Poems like 'Filling Station' and 'The Raising of Lazarus' are inspired by paintings and reinforce the sense of Boran's being an observer. He has the poet's trick of suddenly using language in a strikingly refreshing way. 'How To Be My Heart' for instance, ends memorably with: "Make haemoglobin/ while the sun shines. / But keep a little oxygen aside."

Graham Hartill's *Cennau's Bell* has generous selections from collections produced over twenty years, many of his poems located in Welsh landscapes. These poems have an experimental boldness. Hartill is like a painter: he places his words with care on the blank page for their visual impact. And he is not afraid to leave plenty of blank white spaces. The impact of classical Chinese poetry is evident in his work, yet his poetry is far from being traditional. Here, for instance, is one stanza, question 327 from the prose-poem '1001 Things To Ask Of Any City': "How many calories could you find in the average dust-bin?"

Monologues are an important feature of *Cennau's Bell*. The opening poem has a Mazatec shaman and healer in Mexico as its persona, while in 'At Cennau's Well' a holy woman communes with Nature:

> and what's this place but a bigger body,
> a musculature of stones and beasts and jungled ridges?

Whatever the name, I am now become this territory.

Celtic mysticism and Shamanistic folklore are also important influences. Whether using the voice of the 7th century English missionary, St Cedd, or that of a Roman soldier's ghost, Hartill's spiritual poems are best read when in a meditative mood.

Piotr Sommer's *Continued* has selections of poetry and prose pieces from his collections dating from 1980. His poems are low-key vignettes of daily life in Poland; nothing exciting happens but sometimes there's an ironic aside or interpretation to some mundane happening. In 'A Maple Leaf' he describes a "maple leaf with the sun shining through it" as "beautiful", but almost immediately has to qualify his words with "but / not excessively so". Sommer is a poet of the small moment: in his poetry the seed contains not just the tree but a whole forest. So one is not surprised to find a short poem inspired by the work of Wang Wei, an eighth century Chinese poet. In 'Indiscretions' he writes of: "syntaxes that pretend that something links them together. / Between these inter-meanings the whole man is contained, / squeezing in where he sees a little space."

In his perceptive 'Foreword' August Kleinzahler calls Sommer "the poet as double agent, working both sides of the border and travelling incognito". He also notes "a quality of otherness in the poetry[...]. Boundaries are continually being crossed" – a remark that rings just as true for the other collections reviewed here.

Debjani Chatterjee's latest collection is *Namaskar: New and Selected Poems* from Redbeck Press. She co-edited *A Slice of Sheffield* (SGMT & Sahitya Press) in 2005.

The Child In Him

DANIEL WEISSBORT

Ted Hughes, *Collected Poems for Children*, illustrated by Raymond Briggs,
Faber, £16.99 hardback, ISBN 0571215017

For Ted Hughes, the literary domain was unbounded. Apart from his own productiveness, far beyond even the work which is generally known – as any visitor to the Hughes archive at Emory University Atlanta can see at once – he was deeply involved in a number of activities, many of them of a public nature, using his position as Poet Laureate to serve various ends, not least that of environmental protection.

He was a visionary poet, rather than a practitioner of art for art's sake, although he was also a formidable craftsman. His production, apart from that of his "own" poems, encompasses drama, translation, essays, and of course writing for children. But he also took an interest in writing by children. With his friend Michael Morpurgo, he was responsible for establishing the post of Children's Laureate, and he was one of the moving forces behind the Daily Mirror Children's Literary Competition, which published the "Children as Writers" anthologies for a number of years from the late 1950s. Hughes's particular concern with the teaching of literature took the form of frequent visits to schools and, among other things, a series of BBC broadcasts, collected in *Poetry in the Making* (Faber, 1967), for the series "Listening and Writing". This includes an anthology of poems, the nucleus of his contribution to the anthology of poems, for children and others, *The Rattle Bag* (Faber, 1982, co-edited with Seamus Heaney). The Arvon Foundation courses – a bold innovation in this country, where poetry workshops had traditionally been regarded with suspicion – have by now encouraged generations of young and not-so-young writers.

It is not easy to review a book by Ted Hughes because everything here leads into everything else. His own work and the projects which he promoted with selfless energy flow together. But I shall try to keep to the point! It is perhaps this selflessness that commends Hughes's work to children. He was an inspired educator, the best teachers being those who engage their pupils' natural curiosity, who are as interested in them as they themselves are in learning about the world. And so in his own writing for children he never talks down to them – that "for" sounds condescending, but Hughes never is. He himself learnt from children. The child in him remained alive and it is perhaps this, above all, that accounts for the lucidity of his writing, whether for adults or for children. As he says: "Before the pen moves over the paper, the writer's imaginative re-creation of what is to be written must be [...] as if real" (*Winter Pollen*, Faber, 1994, p. 25). So, while he switches gears to some extent when he has a child audience in mind, there is no difference in kind; the humour, often grimly evident (notably in *Crow*, Faber, 1970), is also evident in his writing for children, less grimly but no less forcefully.

But Hughes recognized as well that good writing doesn't just depend on native talent: it is the result of effort, of discipline comparable to that advocated by Loyola (see the essay 'A Word about Writing in Schools', *Winter Pollen*). In his anthology *By Heart, 101 Poems to Remember* (Faber, 1997) he includes by way of introduction his essay 'Memorising Poems', which advocates memorising as a way not just of training the memory – in itself a vital discipline – but of personally owning, as it were, memorable poems.

There is much more to be said, but what it boils down to is this. The collection of Ted Hughes's *Collected Poems for Children* is a volume all should have. It is a source of endless pleasure and I use that word advisedly. In it Hughes is revealed as a celebrator of nature, in all its aspects, and of language, which is a part of nature. His humour, utterly honest and spot-on, is also loving. In *Under the North Star*, for instance (first published by Faber in 1981 with drawings by the late Leonard Baskin), Hughes ends 'Mooses' with the line: "Two dopes of the deep woods". There are innumerable other examples of his ability to combine loving humour and descriptive precision.

So, here is a book equally for children and adults, with or without children. It is wittily and inventively illustrated by Raymond Briggs, which adds to its attractiveness; although I personally found the illustrations occasionally distracting and sentimental, whereas Hughes is never distracted and never succumbs to sentimentality. His poems for children not only enter the world of children but are an invitation to children to enter the world about them and to engage creatively with it and with what should and must interest them if we are to survive as a species. I do not think that is an exaggerated claim.

The poet and translator Daniel Weissbort co-founded *Modern Poetry in Translation* with Ted Hughes in 1966. His *From Russian With Love* is reviewed in *Poetry Review* 95:4.

❧

Quivering Eros

SIMON SMITH

Kenneth Koch, *The Collected Poems*, Knopf, $40.00, ISBN 1400044995

Kenneth Koch's *The Collected Poems*, a mammoth celebration running to 761 pages, is the perfect opportunity to witness the development of a great poet's work over fifty-odd years of a writing career. Other commentators have seen the sweep and shape of Koch's oeuvre as one starting with experiment, gradually transforming into a personal voice, which eventually achieves a new fluency in the elegiac. *The Collected Poems* bears out this pattern; however, all the poems have in common a sophisticated urbanity. They somehow hover above the experiences taking place, whilst being a part of them too; a simultaneity of fun and intellection which can sometimes make Koch seem like a French poet writing in (American) English.

Koch's reputation has suffered for several reasons. He moved too quickly, too mercurially, for observers to keep up: he was fiction writer, playwright, academic and teacher as well as poet. His workshops at the New School for Social Research in New York helped shape a second generation of New York poets; but most surprising was his pioneering and innovative work with young children and the elderly in the 1960s and 1970s. He created a pedagogy and practice for these groups of the poetically dispossessed virtually single-handed. And this excellent work has meant the seriousness of his own poetry has been overlooked; this, and the apparent lightness, the comedy, the who-framed-roger-rabbit quality of the slap-stick, ridiculous rhyme and ill-advised, not to say precipitous, use of "dead" verse forms.

If Frank O'Hara is New York's Shelley, whose neo-Romanticism and experimentation travels between the white noise and Abstract Expressionist "Second Avenue" and his streetwise I-do-this-I-do-that poems; then Koch is its Lord Byron. Koch's poetry is Romantic, comic and, most importantly, neo-Classical. But, just as Byron reins-in a wayward Romantic sensibility in strict verse forms, so Koch reins-in the vernacular impulsiveness that opens this *Collected* in *Sun Out: Selected Poems 1952-54*. Later, he uses similarly Byronic verse forms as a platform to launch into ambitious and discursive longer poems. Koch's uncertainties about these early, exuberant experiments remained almost until the end: he didn't publish *Sun Out* until 2000.

But Allen Ginsberg once declared Frank O'Hara American poetry's Catullus. And perhaps Koch is New York's Ovid and, maybe, its Horace; he calls two of his own extended poems 'The Art of Love' and 'The Art of

Poetry', a nod in the direction of both Ancients. And it is neo-Classical urbanity which is the most constant strand of Koch's poetry; where its intellectual sense of humour rises into a form of Eros, a form of desire that threatens to break the mind's control. The poetry which grows out of the collection *Thank You*, particularly that of *The Pleasures of Peace* and *The Art of Love*, never ceases to be analytical, yet can achieve a quivering moment of Eros through antic wit. Many of the "list" poems, like 'Sleeping with Women', achieve a similar unrelenting, irresistible, stroboscopic erotic state through repetition.

However the greatest, and pivotal, example of this transformation comes in the title poem of 'The Pleasures of Peace'. Here the poet enters a conversation with "the Professor", a comic Jerry Lewis-like figure, who opines: "'I think [the poem] adequately encompasses the hysteria of our era.'" And then this happens:

> The Professor paused, lightly, upon the temple stair.
> 'I will mention you among the immortals, Ken,' he said,
> 'Because you have the courage of what you believe.
> But there I will never mention those sniveling rats
> Who only claim to like these things because they're fashionable.'
> 'Professor!' I cried, 'My darling! My dream!' And she stripped, and I saw there
> Creamy female marble, the waist and thighs of which I had always dreamed.
> 'Professor! Loved one! Why the disguise?' 'It was a test' she said,
> 'Of which you have now passed the first portion.
> You must write More, and More – '
> 'And be equally persuasive?' I questioned, but She
> Had vanished through the Promontory door.

This Ovidian metamorphosis of mental activity into erotica – a version of Orpheus and Eurydice – also draws on the comic-book world of the contemporary sixties classic comedy *How to Murder your Wife*, in which screen goddess Virna Lisi emerges from a cake at a bachelor party to marry the erstwhile drunk played by Jack Lemmon. Lemmon's comedy is to find his goddess and regret it straight away. Koch's is a more complicated, troubled and darker process, carried out through loss rather than discovery, where the Professor/goddess is revealed in a form of sexless intellection; the poem takes part in both these worlds of the (distant) mythic and the (immediate) comic, only to have its object disappear into thin air.

Commentaries on Koch's work have concentrated on the chaotic qualities and nervous crackle of the verse's pace, veering dangerously towards loss of control. But the tempered urbanity revealed in the final two books, *New Addresses* and *A Possible World*, finally flowers in the poet's heart-breaking and brave realisation of his own mortality. *New Addresses* hails the impending loss of Self to aging through a whole series of objects, ideas and emotional states to be addressed, reconciled and realised. Perhaps the most moving of these poems is 'To World War Two', where the elderly poet addresses the War itself, like an ungrateful lover, through his younger self, the G.I.: "I who had gone about for years as a child / Praying God don't let there ever be another war / Or if there is, don't let me be in it. Well, I was in you. / All you cared about was existing and being won. / You died of a bomb blast in Nagasaki, and there were parades." There are few better poems about the Second World War.

Kenneth Koch's *Collected Poems* is not only a testimony to his importance within the New York School, but enhances his position as one of the half dozen or so great American poets to come to prominence in the latter half of the twentieth century. The book's closing words sum up the opening out, the humility and humanity the reader experiences by reading *The Collected Poems*: "This existence like another / taking place."

Simon Smith is Librarian of the Poetry Library. His latest collection is *Mercury* (Salt, 2006).

℘

Understating the Case

HELENA NELSON

Clare Pollard, *Look, Clare! Look!*, Bloodaxe, £7.95, ISBN 1852247096;
Jane Duran, *Coastal*, Enitharmon, £8.95, ISBN 1900564246

It's a mixed blessing being hailed as a "young poet", which is what has happened to Clare Pollard ever since she burst onto a scene of predominantly middle-aged to elderly UK poets in 1998. But a line in *Look, Clare! Look!* declares she was "born twenty-five years ago". Well – Keats was dead at twenty-six – it's clearly high time to regard Pollard as grown-up. And there are some poems here (as indeed in her previous two books) where you simply think "this is good", without adding as a kind of patronising afterthought "for her age".

However, this is not true of all her work; and though this is not a long collection, some of the contents do Pollard no favours. The book opens with a travel sequence: poems from China, Cambodia, Vietnam, Laos, Thailand, Burma, New Zealand, Australia, Fiji and America. The remarks on each country fit neatly inside the *Look, Clare! Look!* umbrella, and if she had been content to do just that – to look, and not draw conclusions – the set might have been colourful, if unexceptional. But she swings incongruously from ingenuous teenage-style commentary ("Amongst our favourite things in Australia are the Big things, / which are just these huge, huge things, basically, / like a Big Rocking Horse, say, / or a Big Mango") to a rather ponderous Prufrock-on-vacation: "But I have seen the traps they left for those children…"

Then suddenly there is 'Mission Beach', the last of the world-tour sequence. Abandoning "asides" on international inequalities, Pollard evocatively records skinny-dipping with her boyfriend, swimming – without knowing it – in "stinger season", when both might have been hurt or killed. This personal relationship sits at the heart of a book in which love and loss offset each other. All credit to the boyfriend (later to become husband) for the delightful hand-drawn map which shows him with backpack and t-shirt subtitled "The Muse", while Pollard stands as "the Poet" in the other corner holding a gigantic quill pen. This is touching and funny. But I think he really *is* her muse: many of the best poems feature him. 'For My Fiancé' is a lovely piece of writing. 'For the Other Ones', another love poem, has lyrical clarity, and 'Cordelia at the Service Stop', which features (I think) the Muse as the person who "needed the loo", is magnificent. It's understated, moving and an expert marriage of form and feeling.

When Pollard cuts back, she can be first-rate. The first eighty-five lines of 'My Father and the Snow', though self-evidently important to their author and the story she wants to tell, seem to me to be less than essential. The last seventeen (which I think could stand on their own) bring tears to my eyes.

Jane Duran is a very different poet: her language is intensely restrained and spare. In fact, the drawback to such understated art is that some poems can seem slight enough to disappear, unless the reader is reading every bit as carefully as Duran herself writes.

Coastal centres on two events: first the illness and subsequent death of the poet's mother; secondly, the joyful relationship with her newly-adopted baby son. There is sadness here, but overall it's a warmly celebratory book. At first I felt some of the titles a little heavy – pieces titled 'Stroke' and 'Dementia' are baldly obvious, compared to the subtly textured content. But later I was glad of their simplicity. The poems are graceful and almost elusive; they move slowly and meticulously; the line breaks delay (but don't fracture) the syntax. In a poem from Duran's first book (*Breathe Now, Breathe*) she described how she had "fallen asleep / after a few lines of a poem / have come to me, / the breath of a poem / I had not understood till now". That sense persists here – the feeling that each poem has "come to her", like a gift she is sharing with the reader. The language, though characteristically plain, has haunting resonance. The title poem 'Coastal' illustrates this neatly:

> I know each moment –
> stories that wash up
> coasts that take and take the light,
> the first beaten-back mornings.

The "take and take", like the ocean, has depth. In many pieces, Duran accomplishes a sharp reality out of all proportion to the simplicity of her diction. In 'Streetlife', for example, she records the activity of hanging out the washing in a hot Algerian city where water is at a premium. Each line sketches in a detail until the poem swells to something bigger than itself, the final words an astonishing climax.

For me, in the end, the highlight is one individual lyric. It is exceptionally beautiful – the sort of poem you feel you've somehow always known. It isn't easy to quote in part, though it's more sonorous and less understated than the rest. Each of the five plangent stanzas completes the title 'There Are Women'. Here are the last two:

> Who stand still when the tide overcomes
> their large bare feet. Who muddle their sex,
> their struggle. Who come in close to him,
>
> whose faces are so close there is nowhere to hide.
> Women for whom I would take the combs
> from my hair and weep openly, face to face.

Helena Nelson is editor of *Sphinx* and runs the poetry chapbook imprint HappenStance Press (www.happenstancepress.com).

ॐ

DOROTHY SARGENT ROSENBERG ANNUAL POETRY PRIZES, 2006

Prizes ranging from $1,000 up to as much as $25,000 will be awarded for the finest lyric poems celebrating the human spirit. Entries are due November 6, 2006.

The contest is open to all writers, published or unpublished, who will be under the age of 40 on that date. Only previously unpublished poems are eligible for prizes. Notice of prize winners will be published on our website on February 5, 2007.

Please visit our website: www.DorothyPrizes.org for further information and to read poems by previous winners.

Checklist of Contest Guidelines

* Entries must be postmarked on or before November 6, 2006.
* Submissions must be in English: no translations, please.
* Each entrant may submit one to three separate poems.
* Only one of the poems may be more than thirty lines in length.
* Each poem must be printed on a separate sheet.
* Submit two copies of each entry with your name, address, phone number and email address clearly marked on each page of one copy only.
* Include an index card with your name, address, phone number and email address and the titles of each of your submitted poems.
* Include a $10 entry fee payable to the Dorothy Sargent Rosenberg Memorial Fund. (The fee is waived for entrants mailing from foreign countries)
* Poems will not be returned. Include a stamped addressed envelope if you wish us to acknowledge the receipt of your entry.

Mail entries to:

Dorothy Sargent Rosenberg Poetry Prizes,
PO Box 2306, Orinda,
California 94563

ENDPAPERS

Maybe it *is* hopeless and naïve to read and write poetry in Skopje, Macedonia, where you can talk about politics with everyone, and about poetry with hardly anyone.

      — Magdalena Horvat

LETTER FROM SKOPJE

MAGDALENA HORVAT

I'm leafing through a book, the way you're supposed to when visiting a book fair. It's no ordinary book; it's one of January's bestsellers, according to the organiser of the previous such literary trade event that ended a week ago. Yes, I know: two book fairs in Skopje already, and it's only February!

The first fair was a popular affair, judging by the coverage it got in the papers and by its reported sales of over 20,000 books. You'd be hard pressed, however, to find *poetry* among the sought-after titles. The only poet mentioned was Mateja Matevski with his *Collected Works*. "He's exceptional," I nodded reading the article, not least because I've used his lines as the epigraph to my first collection:

> Where do you come from, where to, you familiar unforgettable
> song you hopeless child you naïf…

Maybe it *is* hopeless and naïve to read and write poetry in Skopje, Macedonia, where you can talk about politics with everyone, and about poetry with hardly anyone. But I'm hopeless and naïve enough to do it. I've also been fortunate enough to grow up reading Matevski, as well as Kočo Racin, Blaže Koneski, Aco Šopov, Radovan Pavlovski, Mihail Rendžov, Svetlana Hristova-Jocik, Olga Arbuljevska – to name but a few poets from our 20th century literary canon. Most are still alive and writing well. Racin, Koneski and Šopov passed on. Even so, they feature high on people's favourite-poet lists, if not on the bestseller ones.

I know because I asked. Poets, publishers, readers, even non-readers. The last group was unanimous in saying: "People can't enjoy poetry because of other priorities, like getting food on the table." Others said: "If you wanted to, you *could* spend 100 denars [£1] on a book!" Another reader from Skopje mentioned Koneski, Racin, Šopov, Gane Todorovski and Slavko Janevski among his favourites. The last poetry book he'd bought was Marko Petruševski's *A Confused Young Man* (Az-buki, 2001). "I also read [the online magazine] Blesok and poetry blogs," he adds. "Blogging will change the way artists find their audience. Poetry can be popular. There is a readership. But publishers don't do much to promote poetry. Even Lidija Dimkovska is more familiar to me for her novel *Candid Camera* than for her poems."

Dimkovska, whose *Do Not Awaken Them With Hammers* (Ugly Duckling Press) will come out in the USA this year, feels that Macedonian poetry isn't promoted enough abroad: "I could count on my fingers the number of Macedonian poets published in other languages during the last decade. I wouldn't blame foreign indifference so much as I blame Macedonian literary politics." Her poetry has been influenced by "Macedonian folk songs, Koneski, Pavlovski, Šopov, Todorovski," and she enjoyed "the recent collections by Katica Kulavkova, Risto Lazarov, Jovica Ivanovski and Nikola Madžirov".

Madžirov, whose latest book was *In the City, Somewhere* (Magor, 2004) and whose work-in-progress is titled *Displaced Stone*, apologised for being unable to mention favourites. As for the current scene, Madžirov says, "Macedonian poetry has that constant number of readers which Enzensberger speaks of, regardless of the country's size. There's a continual lack of verbal and video presentation, though, before publication."

Asked whether this is a good time for poetry, Olga Arbuljevska, whose first collection since 1991, *Lifeline*, is upcoming from Makedonska Reč, says: "There's never a good or bad time for poetry. True, the literary magazines are dying out. Literary criticism is almost nonexistent. Writers are at the tail end of priorities – but poetry can, and should, be written."

Toše Ognjanov, a journalist on the paper *Dnevnik*, agrees that the exposure poetry gets isn't enough. "Publishers are interested in profit. Poetry is considered non-commercial. Editors rarely allow space for poetry news, because supposedly it won't draw readers." Still, Ognjanov enjoyed Kulavkova's *Blind Angle* (Kultura, 2004), and among his favourites counts Vlada Uroševik and, of course, Koneski.

This year marks the 85th anniversary of the great Blaže Koneski's birth, and the Struga Poetry Evenings festival, which is in its 45th year, will honour him by raising a statue in Struga's Poetry Park this August. The largest poetry festival in South East Europe – despite the Ministry of Culture's budget cuts – will, as is traditional, publish a dozen poetry books. SPE's president Zoran Ančevski says, "The festival miraculously managed to save itself from the Balkan havoc in the past fifteen years of transition, especially in the past five years of merciless politicisation of everything in this country." But Ančevski doesn't think the Ministry of Culture, the media and publishers encourage writers. "The poet is discouraged by all those factors. In Macedonia, there isn't an infrastructure up to the task of presenting writers and their works. Most publishers only transfer state funds to the authors and behave like usurers, retaining a good percentage of those funds."

A look at this year's Ministry-sponsored books list reveals few poetry titles. Nove Cvetanoski, who runs Makedonska Reč, says: "Some publishers aren't interested in poetry. It's not lucrative. But it doesn't mean it isn't read. Most likely, Makedonska Reč will publish the highest number of poetry titles – by Arbuljevska, Ivica Čelikovik, Jordan Danilovski, Trajče Kacarov, Emil Kaleškovski, and a three-part anthology – in time for the annual book fair in May."

But back to the fair in the Cultural-Informative Centre, a sprawling three-storey building also known as The Workers' University. I learnt English in its classrooms, two flights up. Now I find myself in a ground floor gallery. Stacks of books cover tables not unlike restaurant ones: white tablecloths and everything.

Surprised at the setting, I approach the *pi*-shaped row of improvised bookstands. I scan the titles. Books like *Who Moved My Cheese?* seem prevalent. Some novels, old and new. I leaf through the bestseller I mentioned at the beginning of this letter: a politician's love story. I put it back. Next, I pass children's books. Dictionaries. Here and there, a book on literary theory.

"Any poetry?" I ask each salesperson.

Some of them smile and say they have this or that book, but unfortunately haven't brought it along. Some offer me collections I already have. Some, matter-of-factly, say: "No." And then – a miracle happens!

Rilke's *Duino Elegies* and *Sonnets to Orpheus*, in Macedonian.

I blink in astonishment.

The book I'd searched for in every bookshop this summer, to no avail – so that later I had to translate the 'Fourth Elegy' (from three English versions) for an informal Rilke reading near Duino last July. I got away with it, in case you're wondering; probably because I was the only Macedonian speaker there! But seeing four copies of this 1983 edition, translated by Dušan Tomovski from the German – and kept in some storage box, to be ultimately placed on a white tablecloth for me to find – would've brought tears of joy to my eyes, were I prone to such things.

Instead, I reached for my wallet and bought the least battered copy. And now, if you'll excuse me, I'll get back to Rilke's *Elegies* and Liszt's *Consolations*. Even though, as Ashbery writes, "I've never been consoled by them. Well, once maybe."

Magdalena Horvat recently completed her first collection, *This Is It, Your* (forthcoming from Makedonska Reč, 2006). The webmaster of ThePoem.co.uk, a journalist and translator, she's currently translating Pat Boran's *New and Selected Poems* (reviewed on p.99).

Letter to the Editor

John Kinsella writes in the current *Poetry Review* [95:4], "I do not want my poems to give pleasure". I do not know how many readers of poetry – be they practitioners or not – are happy with the idea of a pleasureless poetry. But, at least, John Kinsella has precisely articulated why scarcely any contemporary poetry sells and reaches a large audience, if most of its practitioners share his aim; and why it is an art that has to be propped up by grants and subsidies.

To guarantee this non-giving of pleasure (*dulce et decorum non est!*), Kinsella desires his poems to be uncomfortable and non-telling, and "to suggest and to bother – to irritate and instigate". Are we here hearing the voice of academia? The profound acceptance of the teacher that learning must always be a stiff, a solemn and, ultimately, miserable affair? Proof – if proof were now needed – that poetry is no longer an art that actually appeals in its own right, but simply has become downgraded (or upgraded depending on your view) to an aid to teaching? Or is it something more peculiar still, like a celebratory [*sic*] chef insisting all his meals be made of putrid ingredients?

WILLIAM OXLEY, BRIXHAM

Jane Holland
Deciphering The Rejection Letter

Doc Ian
Thankly for these homely carrot honeyful pies.
In rally arry I woolit quit loot ay in –
oh fell I've hit a too lorry.
Plare de sil rue!
Very wisest, Feng Shui.

Door Jam
Thoroughly for these only correct bountiful yams.
I'm roulley army I woubbit quilt fot any is –
al fch I've hid a too loony.
Plane di ail muc!
Very wormey, Frère Lecteur.

Dour Jim
Thankway for these oily concrete lentiful pores.
I'm really angry a rabbit quiet fat again –
if such I'll hole a too lazy.
Please don't send more!
Very worst, In Horror.

Dear Jane
Thank you for these lovely concise? beautiful poems.
I'm really sorry I couldn't quite fit any in –
and feel I've held on too long.
Please <u>do</u> send more!
Very warmest, The Editor.

That's enough. – Ed.

EDITORIAL

Give us bread, but give us roses.
                    – James Oppenheim

Bread and roses, the necessary and the beautiful, come out of *the land*. But where is that land? Is it something local? Global? In our urban culture, land no longer means a daily experience of placed-ness. Nor, luckily, does it mean a particular kind of unmitigated locality: such as the being-in-the-right-place which Martin Heidegger offered as a philosophical groundwork for National Socialism.

Cities disrupt this pull of the local, the mono-cultural or the frankly racist, as both sides of that struggle – the *Volkdeutsch* no less than the cosmopolitan Modernists – always knew they did. John Berger, two of whose essays appeared in our last issue, records this disruption in his great trilogy *Into Their Labours*. The alienation of the peasant-farmer who becomes a slum-dweller consists in no more or less than the alienation of labour. It's a migration from the dignity – however painful, however pitiful – which comes with some control of the working day, to the anomie of unemployment or casual mechanised labour.

So Rose Schneiderman's suffrage polemic, made famous by Oppenheim in his Labour Movement anthem, yokes these elements of necessity and meaning together. Still producing a small thud of surprise after all these years, "bread and roses", in combination, become concrete and particular. Just like Louis MacNeice's bay-window, "Spawning snow and pink roses against it". It's juxtaposition that works this magic: redeeming bread, roses, snow, from lonely symbolic existence. The same trick of sympathetic magic is at work in that earliest metaphor, the charm. Ioana Ieronim brings a traditional Romanian sequence to life in this issue of *PR*: while Richard Burns records how metaphor also turns one thing into another elsewhere in the Balkans, in the *dodola* rainmaking rituals of the former Yugoslavia.

If this issue of *Poetry Review* goes "back to the land", it is frequently to the land-mass of the European continent. "European Landscapes" include not only the Romanian *descantece* but work from Czech neo-pastoralist Petr Borkovec and the senior Slovak Mila Haugová. For her, the female body is the suffering "ground" on which we all move. But of course most of the writing in this issue is from the English-speaking world: wherever that begins and ends. And much of it deals with the confusing subject of placement, "Arrowing In" not only on St Andrews and Naples, the Mexican desert and the coast of Thailand, but to the human self. While Amarjit Chandan wants to live with and through his beloved, Yang Lian's searching 'Journey' towards a home-in-exile returns us to the metaphysical dilemmas beyond concrete apprehension.

We live in radical geophysical times. But what does a poetry which responds to ecological challenge look like? Pastoral won't do, as Raymond Williams pointed out in *The Countryside and the City*. It's simply *faux* nostalgia for something un-experienced; a city-dweller's fantasy. Polemic, meanwhile, is one good way to murder a poem.

Yet poets do find ways to attend to the ecological. W. S. Merwin steps in to the shamanic. John Kinsella's poetic persona is *Pan*-ic, encouraging the challenge and chaos of the actual to disrupt the learnt cadences of conventional poetics. Allison Funk gives a lyric, caretaking attention to the what-is. Poetries which pay a deep-level attention to the land cut no ideological corners; are widely differentiated; but seem to share certain strategies of resistance – to the facile, the ready-made. They continue, we might say, to work the palpable: to offer us *what's here*.

FIONA SAMPSON

PR
JUKEBOX

Poetry Review Jukebox is a chance to replay high points from the journal's past. Requests, for material from issues published before 1995, are welcomed.

As we celebrate the Geoffrey Dearmer Prize winner in this issue, here is Dearmer's own reflection on the poetry of his contemporaries, from *PR* 51:1, Jan-Mar 1960...

Geoffrey Dearmer
'Ah, Did You Once See ...'

Gentle Reader, we beg your indulgence
If you find in *The Poetry Review*
A lack of new forms of effulgence:
Can you wonder, I put it to you?

Reflect how the Great Global Noises
Big Worthwords and Whitmen and such,
All the wavelengths they've filled with their voices,
And what's left for us isn't much.

We're reduced to ungentlelike scrimmages
To scrape what is left of the rhymes,
For they've bagged all the obvious images
And rung all the changes and chimes.

Theirs was the muckle, ours is the mickle;
Parnassus was glorious and green
When they reaped with the scythe and the sickle
Where we, like poor Ruth, have to glean.

Yet we needn't despair of the weather,
Nay rather, like Browning, with pride
Pick up from the heather and Eagle's feather
    A Moulted feather
And lay it our breasts inside.

...and a younger poet of today reading one of the poets of the 1960s...

Kit Fan
Reading Thom Gunn's Notebooks
At The Bancroft Library

for H. H.

Let's talk about Gunn.
Not *Thom*, not the one haunted by Charlotte
Thomson Gunn since she gassed
herself when he was fifteen.
(See 'The Gas Poker' in *Boss Cupid.*)

But *Gunn*, the anonymous.
'The dead poet.' 'The Prince of Cats.' Not nine
lives but one. '*Who am I / speaking to /
in this poem if / you are not here?*'
'Here' being this seat at the edge

of this table, from the window
all this green sharpens under the sun – redwood,
eucalyptus. It is finally California.
'*How hard is it for me / to believe
being / in this place when / I am already / here?*'

('Along the Simplon's steep
and rugged road'.) The campanile strikes – *one* –
from a distance it looks like the one
in *Piazza San Marco* in Venice –
(*sshh)* listen, it strikes again – *one.*

Twice, hourly, turning
the pages back. The first cyclotron and
plutonium; californium and berkelium;
the first sketches for the atomic
bomb *here* among these emerging groves.

Read on.
It's a question of Gunn and his notebooks
as manuscripts mean handwriting
     mean a presence of someone
          long gone but now '*here*' again

     hissing on these pages.
'Hissing', not yet speaking, like the tail of a cobra
cautious long enough, about to strike.
     It's nearing five. The clouds
          have just come in near the campanile.

     They too, are about
to strike. *One, one.* A click, a raindrop.
This divided country where the two sides
     of its continent cannot look up
          but hear the growing emptiness within.

     '*Tell me if you can /*
what is / within / you?' 'You' being neither a *Thom*
nor a *Gunn;* being the *you* you know the best,
     the *you* like most *yous* are, whatever
          they mean in different circumstances.

     What is *within* you
that makes you lie on the floor at home alone,
and think of pills, high buildings, a
     river, car crash or heart attack?
          What makes you time the untimely act?

     It must be nearing five.
'*Why do I / always think / ahead / of time even though / it*
has no / head or tail?' The library's closing
     early for 'seismic renovation'. '*The moving*
          ground; / these manuscripts / above soft vibrations?'

     '*Here* it is a mix
of sunshine and hail, wild light bursts and knife-
like gusts of wind.' You wrote in an email,
     'I have planted salad, rocket, parsley,
          spinach and even a couple of tomato plants.

But otherwise
have been reading, writing, playing Beethoven
and Shostakovitch on the piano.' I walk out
      of the library, pass the campanile.
           It's good to think of your hands digging

      in the soil and piano.
'Isn't it supposed / to be about Gunn / and his notebooks?'
On the platform for the Bay Area, there's
      a man who opens his palms to the sky,
           follows me into the coach and sits opposite.

      He sings, he murmurs.
He's talking to me. *'Why is it / hailing / in May?'*
He opens his palms; he glares at me,
      humming something resembling
           human speech: 'I know you don't smile,

      you don't speak.
But that's the way I get to know you. You know
I'm all on my own.' *'Is it democracy / when
      there is no / one to vote / for?'* I've to look
           away. 'What makes / you stop / writing but go on drinking /*

      and picking up homeless / junkie
boys for / your bed?' You don't stop. *'Will there be a last / salmon?'*
You open your palms. *'Wasn't that an earthquake / or a bomb?'*
      'Hasn't the bell / struck?' Again to the sky. *'What
           is / left to read?'* 'Tell me / why / why the bell / is still /still?'*

National Poetry Competition 2005

First prize

Melanie Drane
The Year The Rice-Crop Failed

The year we married, rainy season lasted
so long the rice crop failed. People gave up
trying to stay dry; abandoned umbrellas
littered the streets like dead birds. One evening
that summer, a typhoon broke the waters
of the Imperial moat and sent orange carp flopping
through the streets around the train station,
under the feet of people trying to go home.
The stairs to the temple became impassable;
fish slid down them in a waterfall, heavy
and golden as yolks. That night, I woke you
when the walls of our home began to shake;
we held our breath while the earth tossed,
counted its pulse as though we could protect
what we'd thought would cradle us –
then the room went still and you moved away,
back into sleep like a slow swimmer,
your eyes and lips swollen tight with salt.
The next morning, a mackerel sky hung over Tokyo.
The newspaper confirmed the earthquake
started inside the sea. I watched you dress to leave,
herringbone suit, shirt white as winter, galoshes
that turned your shoes into small, slippery otters.
After you were gone, I heard hoarse and angry screams;
a flock of crows landed on the neighbor's roof,
dark messengers of Heaven. Did they come to reassure,
to tell me we'd be safe, that we would find
our places no matter how absurd it seemed,
like the fish sailing through the streets,
uncertain, but moving swiftly?

Dominic McLoughlin

I Do Wish Someone Would Ask Me To The Races With Him/Her

Ridiculous to think at twenty three
I used to wear a hot pink tee shirt
and one dangly black earring

to the typing school in Mayfair.
I was the only guy in the class except
for one man three weeks ahead of me

with a very fast w.p.m.
Key learning strategy: don't
look at the keyboard, look at the facsimile

of the keyboard we have placed on your desk.
Helpful tip: keep both feet on the ground.
By week two we had to type full sentences

I must buy a new pair of black stockings.
When we graduated with capable fingers,
on a gorgeous spring day a classmate asked me –

by the bus stop at Speakers' Corner –
if I would go to the races with her.
She had an encyclopaedic knowledge of blood-stock

and conditions of the turf. I said no,
thinking these things inevitably lead to trouble
with one's girlfriend. Little men in silk.

Hot flanks in the winner's enclosure.
Peering through binoculars, mouthing
an unlikely name from the card.

Third prize
Kevin Saving
Dog Otter

He senses danger and is gone,
the water bulging in his wake.
You needn't ever count upon
this sight again, and so should take
the memory and then move on...

You'll never know what rendezvous he'll break
with liquid arabesques – nor how he'll trawl
fresh eddys, find new shoals to dredge.
His underwater playgrounds call
within him like a lover's pledge.
He'll wear the river like a shawl
in slicked-back freedom, near the water's edge.

All the winning poems were published in the *Independent on Sunday,* media
partners of the National Poetry Competition since 2001, on 12 March 2006.

Poetry Review is glad to follow the annual tradition of publishing the
three winning poems from the Poetry Society's National Poetry
Competition. In this, its twenty-eighth year, the judges were Alison
Brackenbury, Bernardine Evaristo and Mark Ford. The Competition
attracts up to 10,000 entries annually; and this year in addition to the
winners there were nine commendations. First-placed Melanie Drane,
from Durham, North Carolina is the competition's first international
winner. Bernadine Evaristo says, "I love the stunning imagery in the
very visual winning poem, 'The Year the Rice Crop Failed'; and 'I do
wish someone would take me to the races with him/her' still makes me
smile after many readings".

CONTRIBUTORS

Moniza Alvi's latest collection is *How The Stone Found Its Voice* (Bloodaxe, 2005).

Andrew Bailey is the winner of the Geoffrey Dearmer Prize 2005; his poems have appeared in magazines including *Poetry Review, Stride* and *Ambit.* He lives in Chichester.

Paul Batchelor's pamphlet, *To Photograph a Snow Crystal*, will be published in May by Smith Doorstop. The answer to the poem is honeysuckle.

Petr Borkovec has published five collections of poetry, with books in Italian and German. He is the editor of *Literární noviny.*

Wayne Burrows's *Marginalia* appeared from Peterloo in 2001.

Amarjit Chandan has published six poetry collections and two books of essays in Punjabi and one in English: *Being Here* (The Many Press, 2005).

Alfred Corn is an American poet of international reputation, living partly in the UK. His *Contradictons* is published by Copper Canyon (2002).

Robert Crawford's *Selected Poems* was published by Cape in 2005.

Ruth Fainlight's latest collections are *Sheba and Solomon*, with Ana Maria Pachedo (2004), and *Burning Wire* (Bloodaxe, 2002).

Kit Fan, from Hong Kong, lives in the UK and is working on a thesis on Thom Gunn.

Allison Funk, a professor at Southern Illinois University Edwardsville, is the author of three collections of poems, most recently *The Knot Garden* (Sheep Meadow Press, 2002).

Mila Haugová has been translated into more than a dozen languages and published eleven books to date. Her latest collection in English is *Scent of the Unseen* (Arc, 2003).

Jane Holland's first collection was published by Bloodaxe; she edits the Poets on Fire website.

Douglas Houston's third collection is *The Welsh Book of the Dead* (Seren, 2000).

Ioana Ieronim has published twelve books of poetry, as well as volumes of translation. Her latest, bilingual, book is *Kites Over the Mountain.*

John Kinsella's latest books include *The New Arcadia* and *Peripheral Light: New and Selected Poems*, both reviewed on pp. 88-91.

W.S. Merwin has published more than fifteen books of poetry, twenty books of translation, plays, essays and a memoir of his life in *The Lost Upland of the Auvergne.* His many awards include the Bollingen Prize, a Ford Foundation grant, the Ruth Lilly Poetry Prize and fellowships from The Academy of American Poets, the Guggenheim Foundation, the National

Endowment for the Arts, and the Rockefeller Foundation. He is a former Chancellor of The Academy of American Poets.

David Morley's next collection is *The Invisible Kings* (Carcanet, 2007). He directs the Warwick Writing Programme at the University of Warwick. *The Cambridge Introduction to Creative Writing* is forthcoming from Cambridge University Press.

Paul Muldoon is the lyric writer for RACKETT (formed 2004), though he seems more and more to be getting the hang of a reissue 1952 butterscotch Telecaster and butterscotch maracas, also reissue, which he often shakes at inappropriate times. He plays only 3-car garage rock.

Les Murray's *New Collected Poems* was published in 2004 by Carcanet. His prizes include: the Grace Leven Prize (1980 and 1990), the Petrarch Prize (1995), the T.S. Eliot Prize (1996) and Queens Gold Medal for Poetry (1999).

Pascale Petit's *The Huntress* (2005) was shortlisted for the T. S. Eliot Prize.

Peter Sansom is the Editor of The Poetry Business.

Carole Satyamurti's *Stitching the Dark: New and Collected Poems* appeared from Bloodaxe in 2005.

Michael Schmidt is Professor of Poetry at the University of Glasgow, editorial and managing director of Carcanet Press, and editor of *PN Review*. His *Collected Poems* will be published by Smith/Doorstop in 2007.

Myra Schneider's most recent collection is *Multiplying The Moon* (Enitharmon, 2004) and she is co-editor of anthologies of women's poetry including *Images of Women* due this autumn (Second Light Publications/Arrowhead Press).

Penelope Shuttle has published six collections since 1980, a *Selected Poems* (Poetry Book Society Recommendation, 1997), novels, and is co-author of two widely-read prose works, *The Wise Wound* and *Alchemy for Women*.

Gerard Smyth's fifth collection is *A New Tenancy* (Dedalus, Dublin, 2004).

Julian Stannard teaches Creative Writing at the University of Winchester. *The Red Zone* – his second collection – is published by Peterloo later this year.

Matthew Sweeney's latest collection is *Sanctuary* (Cape, 2004).

Mark Weiss who lives in New York, is the author of six books of poetry, coeditor of the anthology *Across the Line / Al otro lado: The Poetry of Baja California*, and editor of the forthcoming *The Whole Island: Six Decades of Cuban Poetry*.

John Hartley Williams's latest collection, *Blues* (2004), was shortlisted for the T. S. Eliot Prize.

Yang Lian's latest collection in English is *Concentric Circles* (Bloodaxe, 2005).